Teddy Bears & Steiff Animals

by
Margaret Fox Mandel

Drawings by Margot Mandel

COLLECTOR BOOKS
A Division of Schroeder Publishing Co., Inc.

The current values in this book should be used only as a guide. They are not intended to set prices, which vary from one section of the country to another. Auction prices as well as dealer prices vary greatly and are affected by condition as well as demand. Neither the Author nor the Publisher assumes responsibility for any losses that might be incurred as a result of consulting this guide.

On the Cover

Light blonde Teddy Bear/red bow, 13″	$650.00 up
Beige mohair Teddy Bear, 10″	675.00 up
Gentle Ben, Mattel black Teddy	55.00
Steiff Dalmatian/crown and cape 6″	250.00 up
Brown Steiff Bear on wheels	700.00 up

(All bears from author's collection)

Dedication

To my daughter, Margot, who encouraged me to collect old Teddy Bears when the finest were selling for $40.00 or less.

Acknowledgements

Acknowledgement is gratefully extended to the following who have graciously shared their toys and photographs.

All photographs are by the author unless noted otherwise in parenthesis.

Joyce M. Al-Khafaji; Carolyn and Dorothy Altfather (Carolyn Altfather); Mary Ann Bonnell; Susan Bowles; Kay Bransky (Art Bransky); Lee Bryant; Susan Buckman; Cecilia Burkhardt; Nanci Burney (herself); Margaret M. Carlson (Dorene J. Fox); Sheri Carter; Nancy Catlin (herself); Anne Chamberlin (herself); Lail Cramm; Terri Dage (herself); Cathy Darden; Pauline M. Davidson; V.M. Davis; Kirsten Deats (Susan Deats); Kate Denious; Denver Museum of Natural History; Tammie Depew (herself); Peg Derry; Brian Dorian (himself); Violet Duncan; Beth Everhart; Barbara J. and George L. Farinsky; Stacie Flanders (Shirlee Glass); Teddy Fonseca; Dorene J. Fox (herself); Herbert Freiberg; Vanita Y. French; Emogene Friant (herself); Diane Gard (herself); Phyllis F. Gilbertson; Shirlee Glass; Violet Goold; Martha Gragg (herself); Mary Grisby; Suelynn Gustafson; Ruby Hinegardner; Diane Hoffman; Linda and Ken Holsworth; Tonja Hoopes; Berdie and Nancy Hupper; Dorothy R. Jones; Virginia Joy (herself); Margaret Klawuhn; Christl Kober; Evelyn Krause (Dwight Smith); Beverly L. Krein; Irma Leaver; Virginia and Floyd Lillard; Wanda Loukides (Roberta Viscusi); Sara McClellan (herself); Carol Matchett; Carolyn, Elizabeth and Hazel Mathews; Marge and Earl Meisinger (David Miller and Earl Meisinger); Bunny Miller; Nan, Pam, Amy, Margaret and Jason Moorehead; Rosemary Moran; Bev, Jim and Tim Murray; Nancy Nelson; Janet Orashan (herself); Randi Parker; David Parrish; Susan Passarelli (David Passarelli); Kayleen Peterson; Deborah Ritchey (herself); Nancy, Susan and Craig Roeder; Ruth L. Ruder (Roe G. Green); Rosella and Tony Santopietro; Ursula Schink (herself); Ernest H. Schroeder; Nanci Schroeder; Louise Schroer; Lenora Schweitzberger; Betty Shelley; Helen Sieverling (Glenn Sieverling); Carol Simons (Janet Orashan); Patricia R. Smith (Dwight Smith); Naomi Stanton; Marian Swartz; Kathy Teske; Evelyn Thomas; Vera Tiger (Virginia Joy); Marge Vance; Wanda Vessels; Roberta Viscusi (herself); Ena Vogel; Marlene Wendt (herself); Ruby B. Wilson; Anita Wright; Darlene Zezula (Virginia Joy).

And above all, to Patricia Smith for her help and encouragement.

Table of Contents

Revised Prices...5
I. Introduction...9
    President Theodore Roosevelt................................10
    Conservation of Teddy Bears.................................10
    Teddy Bears and Children....................................12

II. Teddy Bear Guidelines.......................................13
    What to Look For...14
    Price Guide per Inch.......................................14

III. Margarete Steiff Co., Dolls and Animals.........................15
    Steiff Guidelines, What to Look For..........................17
    Steiff Chronology Table.....................................18

IV. Miniature Teddy Bears.......................................19

V. Teddy Bears Before 1940.....................................37
    1903-1912...38
    1912-1920...79
    1920-1930...99
    1930-1940..131
    Bears on Wheels...160

VI. Teddy Bears, 1940-1980....................................167

VII. Contemporary Teddy Bears..................................199
    Artist Bears..203

VIII. Teddy Bear Related Items..................................207

IX. Steiff Dolls..217

X. Steiff Animals Before 1940.................................227

XI. Steiff Animals, 1940-Present...............................239
    Cats...241
    Dogs...246
    Rabbits..251
    Domestic Animals.......................................253
    Wild Animals and Birds..................................256
    Costumed Animals and Puppets............................285

Teddy Bear Price Guide Revised

Page 20 & 21
Acrobatic Bear.........400.00
Ferriswheel Pair........600.00
Tin Plate...............95.00
Teddy Bear button.......15.00
6" Japanese............35.00
3½" Steiff, 1910........400.00
8" Mohair.............350.00

Page 22 & 23
3¾" Mohair............450.00
5" Hermann............250.00
5" Imported...........150.00
Bathing Bear...........75.00
5½" Bear on Wheels.....25.00
4" Honey Mohair........150.00

Page 24 & 25
Beige Mohair..........400.00
Clown..................25.00
Yellowstone Bear........85.00
Pink Bear..............45.00

Page 26 & 27
Postcards.........10.00-15.00
5½" German Wind-up....45.00
Christmas Ornament.......6.00
2½" Teddy.............25.00
Teddy Bear School.......65.00
Japanese Mini Bears...ea 35.00
6½" Steiff.............275.00
5½" Steiff.............200.00
6" Steiff.............200.00

Page 28 & 29
Walking Bear...........35.00
6" Bear................15.00
Snow White Steiff......350.00
3½" Steiff, left.........300.00
3½" Steiff, right........250.00
Jackie........ 600.00-700.00

Page 30 & 31
Hermann Bears......ea 125.00
6" Dark Mohair........200.00
Young Bear............125.00
The Graduate...........55.00
Drummer...............55.00
7" Petz Bear..........115.00
Wooden Swing..........20.00
Teddy Bear Bottle........20.00

Page 32 & 33
3½" Steiff Teddy.......200.00
White Mohair..........225.00
Beige Mohair..........200.00
6" Teddy Bears...175.00-200.00
Brown Bear............20.00

Page 34 & 35
Oil Cloth Bear.........20.00
Tabby.................35.00
Mohair Bear...........55.00
Snap Bear..............2.00

Page 36
Bisque Doll...........150.00
Total of Bears.........575.00

Page 38 & 39
28" White Mohair.....2,000.00
White Mohair. .3,500.00-4,500.00

Page 40 & 41
16 " Blonde Mohair....1,600.00
13" Stelff.......... 1,600.00
Teddy Bears Book......250.00
16" Gold Mohair......2,000.00

Page 42 & 43
Emerson.............2,500.00
20" Steiff............2,100.00
Dark Brown Steiff......1,300.00
Little Brown Bear Book....65.00

Page 44 & 45
1905 Mohair..........1,100.00
12" Mohair............650.00
Cloth Bear............195.00
13" Mohair............700.00

Page 46 & 47
1907 12" Steiff.........900.00
12" Gold Mohair.......650.00
21" Mohair............600.00
13" Steiff...........1,600.00

Page 48 & 49
Beguiling Bear..........600.00
13" Steiff...........1,300.00
3½" Steiff.............300.00
Blanket................35.00
14" Steiff...........1,400.00
Petsy.................150.00
15" Mohair............800.00

Page 50 & 51
12" Steiff............475.00
14" Mohair...........1,100.00
12" Mohair............700.00

Page 52 & 53
16" Brown Bear........800.00
12" Steiff............800.00
11" Teddy.............600.00

Page 54 & 55
19" Steiff...........1,400.00
14" Mohair............700.00

Page 56 & 57
Lucky.................600.00
14" Steiff...........1,500.00

Page 58 & 59
Twins..............pr. 900.00
Roosevelt Bear........900.00
15" Mohair............100.00
14" Mohair............350.00

Page 60 & 61
10" Steiff............900.00
10" Mohair............900.00
Louie...............1,300.00
15" Mohair............800.00

Page 62 & 63
Steiff Bear............700.00
English Bear..........700.00
12" Steiff............900.00

Page 64 & 65
9½" Mohair............400.00
8" Mohair............300.00
12" Mohair............600.00
Cow, horse & pig....ea. 35.00
Rooster...............55.00
Madonna..............800.00
Child.................350.00

Page 66 & 67
21" Mohair...........1,400.00
22" Mohair...........1,200.00
12" Mohair............900.00
Doll...................50.00
16" Mohair............800.00
Viewer and Cards.......125.00

Page 68 & 69
Grover Cleveland.......800.00

13" Mohair...........900.00
Page 70 & 71
12" Steiff...........1,000.00
12" White Mohair.......650.00
Minerva...............350.00
Bear Boy..............150.00
Fur Bear Boy..........135.00
Tin Horse Cart..........45.00

Page 72 & 73
12" Horsman...........400.00
13" Mohair............700.00
Protective Bear.........550.00
18" Mohair............900.00

Page 74 & 75
Early Bear............900.00
10" Mohair............250.00
12" White Mohair.......250.00
10" Irresistible Bear.....650.00

Page 76 & 77
Smug Bear.............350.00
10" Steiff.............750.00
16" Mohair............800.00
15" Mohair............750.00

Page 78 & 79
21" Mohair...........1,000.00
1915 Steiff, top........1,200.00
1915 Steiff, bottom.....1,200.00

Page 80 & 81
12" Mohair............350.00
17" Mohair............850.00
21" Electric Eye Bear....650.00

Page 82 & 83
22" Electric Eye Bear....625.00
Novelty Bear..........750.00
Patriotic Bear.........600.00
Black Bear............800.00

Page 84 & 85
Steiff Clown Bear.......900.00
24" Mohair............800.00
Book.................185.00
Super Teddy...........750.00
Book..................95.00
Fillmore..............700.00

Page 86 & 87
12" Mohair............450.00
13" Mohair............650.00
11" Mohair............600.00
24" Beige Bear.......1,650.00
Mama Bear............650.00
Papa Bear...........1,800.00
Baby Bear.............175.00

Page 88 & 89
14" Mohair............700.00
14" Steiff...........1,050.00
9" Mohair.............150.00
Poker Face............600.00

Page 90 & 91
Mrs. Roosevelt.........950.00
20" Steiff.............500.00
23" Sailor cloth.........400.00

Page 92 & 93
17" Mohair............500.00
23" American.........1,000.00
10" White Mohair.......300.00
18" Mohair...........1,000.00

Page 94 & 95
Shy Bear..............600.00
Horse.................150.00

Doll's Bear 550.00
Early American Teddy . . . 425.00
Elephant 600.00
Snowball 700.00
Page 96 & 97
18" Mohair 900.00
Teacher 600.00
Book 95.00
21" Mohair 600.00
6" Mohair 200.00
Page 98 & 99
18" Mohair 650.00
14½" Bear 600.00
15½" Bear 700.00
26" Mohair 2,000.00
22" Mohair 650.00
Page 100 & 101
Mechanical Bears . . . . ea. 550.00
Dr. O'Bear 550.00
15" Mohair 450.00
9½" Steiff 700.00
Page 102 & 103
Steiff Clown Bear 600.00
13" Mohair 400.00
Dog 75.00
Bellhop Bear 275.00
Page 104 & 105
13" Mohair 700.00
12" Mohair 700.00
13" Bear 175.00
16" Mohair 400.00
14" Angora Mohair 350.00
Page 106 & 107
24" White Mohair 700.00
20" Mohair 900.00
Sitting dog 125.00
Polish Bear 25.00
Mr. Wheatly 750.00
Page 108 & 109
Old Fellow 350.00
13" Mohair 325.00
Bearskin 20.00
Block 10.00
12" Brown Bear 350.00
Horse 75.00
Donkey 125.00
''See-Saw'' 35.00
Gold Bear 525.00
Page 110 & 111
13" Brown Bear 425.00
23" Mohair 375.00
30" Circus Bear 350.00
22" Circus Bear 75.00
Page 112 & 113
18" Mohair 375.00
16" White Mohair 450.00
16" Gold Mohair 325.00
Trunk 40.00
Mama Bear 175.00
Baby Bear 125.00
16" Golden Mohair 800.00
17" Red Mohair 475.00
Page 114 & 115
Ted 275.00
15" Red, White Blue 500.00
24" Gold Mohair 675.00
Helvetic Bear 1,000.00
18" Mohair 400.00
Page 116 & 117
Pink Mohair 300.00
Red Mohair 200.00
Book 95.00

Brown Mohair 325.00
English Bear 500.00
Book 150.00
Page 118 & 119
21" Mohair 550.00
9" Silver-grey Mohair . . . 675.00
19" Carmel Mohair 550.00
24" Mohair 600.00
Red Coat Bear 550.00
22" Gold Mohair 500.00
Page 120 & 121
20" Gold Mohair 600.00
18" Grey Mohair 550.00
17" White Bear 425.00
16" Telephone Teddy . . . 325.00
17" Telephone Teddy . . . 500.00
15" Thin Bear 450.00
Page 122 & 123
Steam Roller Bear 450.00
Steam Roller 150.00
10" White Mohair 150.00
13" Standing Bear 175.00
12" Seated Bear 175.00
Tuxedo Bear 200.00
Page 124 & 125
Magician 350.00
19" Gold Mohair 375.00
19" Cinnamon Mohair . . . 375.00
16" Gold Mohair 300.00
English Twins . . . . pr. 600.00
Page 126 & 127
12" Gold Mohair 150.00
13" Gold Mohair 85.00
Drum Major 45.00
Twins . . . . pr 550.00
23" Seated Bear 550.00
21" Standing Bear 325.00
12" Younger Bear 125.00
15" Steiff 600.00
Page 128 & 129
Baby Faced Bear 25.00
13" Bear 175.00
Old Timer 300.00
My Teddy 450.00
Page 130 & 131
20" White Mohair 500.00
14" Yellow Mohair 350.00
Green Bear 300.00
Rosie 200.00
14" Pink Bear 300.00
15" Pink Bear 400.00
Page 132 & 133
Undressed 24" Bear 300.00
Dressed 24" Bear 450.00
17" Gold Mohair 350.00
17" Gold Tin Eyes 325.00
12" Teddy 275.00
Page 134 & 135
13" Gold Mohair 250.00
15" Cotton Plush 200.00
Pince Nez Bear 195.00
Roosevelt Pin 35.00
Bear Cart 85.00
19" Cotton Bear 225.00
Older Golliwog 95.00
12" Brown Bear 200.00
Helene 325.00
Page 136 & 137
10" Brown Bear 75.00
14" Orange Bear 85.00
8" Panda 95.00
Waif 400.00

Page 138 & 139
English Panda 325.00
18" Panda 425.00
Steiff from 1950's 450.00
Page 140 & 141
23" Cinnamon Bear 400.00
15" White Mohair 300.00
Book 150.00
23" Cinnamon Bear 250.00
20" Cinnamon Mohair . . . 300.00
Page 142 & 143
Brown Mohair Bear 575.00
English Teddy 550.00
12" Gold Mohair 250.00
Dog 200.00
16" Mohair 275.00
Page 144 & 145
16" Gold Mohair 250.00
12" Gold Mohair 175.00
Fred & Minnie . . . . pr 500.00
Kiss Blowing Bear 275.00
20" Caramel Mohair 300.00
Page 146 & 147
28" Cotton Plush Bear . . . 425.00
Grandpa Bear 275.00
17" White Mohair 250.00
Print 35.00
Page 148 & 149
14" Gold Mohair 300.00
13" White Mohair 200.00
17" Teddy 300.00
12" Bear 275.00
15" White Wool Bear 200.00
Page 150 & 151
Farmer Bear 250.00
Steiff Lamb 150.00
16" Cinnamon Bear 250.00
17" Yellow Mohair 300.00
Dog 95.00
17" White Mohair 300.00
Page 152 & 153
Brown Bear 200.00
Shaggy 250.00
19" Gold Mohair 300.00
Cart 100.00
16" Cinnamon Bear 250.00
Cat 175.00
15" Yellow Mohair 225.00
Brown Mohair 185.00
13" Brown Bear 225.00
Page 154 & 155
Red Riding Hood 150.00
11" Brown Plush Bear 95.00
22" Yellow Mohair 325.00
24" Gold Mohair 350.00
Steiff Puppy 50.00
Cocker Spaniel 50.00
Page 156 & 157
14" Teddy 45.00
21" Pink Bear 250.00
17" White Cotton Plush . . 150.00
Book 50.00
10" Dachshund 85.00
9" Yellow Mohair 135.00
Page 158 & 159
9" Beige Bear 75.00
10" Sandy 125.00
Cloth Doll 50.00
16" Bear 125.00
18" White Wool Bear 150.00
13" Sheepskin Bear 80.00
9" Pink Bear 25.00

6

12½" Younger Bear......75.00	16" Smokey.....55.00	Advertising Bears.ea 20.00-25.00
Wicker Set.....40.00	4¼" Smokey.....10.00	**Page 198**
Page 160 & 161	Punkinheads.....ea. 250.00	Floppy Bear.....150.00
13" Grey Mohair.....225.00	Bear on Wheels.....225.00	**Page 200 & 201**
Bruin Pull Toy.....175.00	1955 Gold Mohair.....275.00	42" Brown Bear.....425.00
Pull Toy Bear...900.00-1,200.00	**Page 180 & 181**	Book, "Misha".....35.00
Page 162 & 163	Black Bear.....150.00	Misha Bears.....per inch 1.50
Riding Bear....900.00-1,200.00	Knickerbocker.....175.00	36" Hermann Bear.....900.00
13" Bear on Wheels.....650.00	19" Gund, 17" Plush..ea 200.00	**Page 202 & 203**
Steiff Pull Toy.....700.00	9" White Mohair.....135.00	Papa Bear.....550.00
Gulliver.....500.00	Reddish-brown Mohair...135.00	Mama and Baby.....350.00
Page 164 & 165	Cuddly Twins.....ea 30.00	Artist Bears.....ea 85.00-125.00
Riding Bear/Pull Toy.....600.00	**Page 182 & 183**	"Debonair Bear," 1st....500.00
10" Bear.....85.00	11" Teddy Baby.....550.00	**Page 204 & 205**
Bear on Wheels.....500.00	Shaggy Brown Mohair...225.00	18" Grey Fur Bear.....120.00
12" Gold Mohair.....475.00	9" Steiff.....75.00	Bellhop Bear.....125.00
Hankie.....10.00	11" Teddy Baby.....600.00	Brown Baby Boy.....100.00
Page 166	21" Grisly.....400.00	20" Artist Bear.....100.00
Pull Toy.....185.00	9" Steiff "Zotty,".....135.00	Running Rabbit.....45.00
9" Teddy Bear.....165.00	8" Steiff Panda.....265.00	Sitting Rabbit.....45.00
Page 168 & 169	15" Steiff "Zotty,".....225.00	**Page 206**
6' Bear.....1,700.00	11" Steiff "Cosy Teddy".110.00	Artist's Bear.....200.00
1941 Steiff Bear.....400.00	10" Hermann.....115.00	"Shirley-o-Bear".....75.00
19" Steiff.....600.00	Steiff Panda Bear.....265.00	Bear Rug.....95.00
Chad Valley.....700.00	9" Panda.....40.00	**Page 208 & 209**
32" Brown Bear.....200.00	**Page 184 & 185**	European Mechanical..1,200.00
34" Gold Bear.....250.00	12" Panda.....20.00	Perfume Bottles.....ea 15.00
29" Gold Bear.....250.00	13" Steiff Panda.....450.00	Perfume Bottle Bear.....375.00
13" Brown/Gold Bear...95.00	12" Black & White Panda.65.00	**Page 210 & 211**
13" Golden Mohair.....200.00	9" Panda Radio.....45.00	Santa Clara Bear.....65.00
Page 170 & 171	13" Plush Panda.....20.00	Teddy Bear Muff.....250.00
15" Gund.....200.00	"Koala Bear".....135.00	Embroidery Work.....350.00
Andy Panda.....95.00	"Zotty".....150.00	Lithograph Blocks.....200.00
Book.....15.00	German Giant.....350.00	Teddy Muff.....200.00
18" Black Bear.....75.00	14" Grey/Beige Wool Bear.75.00	Child's Muff.....150.00
17" Cinnamon Mohair...135.00	5" Japanese Mohair.....25.00	**Page 212 & 213**
Scotch Bearkin.....250.00	**Page 186 & 187**	Oil Panted Photograph...300.00
6" Steiff.....175.00	18" Bear.....90.00	Portrait.....25.00
0" Steiff.....225.00	6" Blond Mohair.....175.00	Child's service.....250.00
3½" Steiff.....225.00	11" Beige Mohair.....45.00	**Page 214 & 215**
21" Spotted Bear.....195.00	18" Steiff.....185.00	Dish.....35.00
Page 172 & 173	11" "Floppy Zotty".....85.00	Toboggan Teddies soap...95.00
9" Beige Steiff.....225.00	6½" "Floppy Zotty".....55.00	Tomato Can.....45.00
11" German Import.....250.00	Hand Puppet.....65.00	Postcards.....ea 10.00-15.00
British Bear.....350.00	**Page 188 & 189**	**Page 216**
Cuddly Bear.....85.00	Dish.....65.00	Inkwell.....95.00
21" Schuco Teddy.....1,150.00	Winnie The Pooh.....75.00	Book.....65.00
13" Schuco Teddy.....700.00	Polar Bear.....150.00	**Page 218 & 219**
Page 174 & 175	22" Wool Bear.....250.00	17" Monkey Man.....2,500.00
22" Schuco.....1,200.00	Christmas Bear.....25.00	Yes/No Bellhop Monkey..275.00
11" Beige Bear.....295.00	**Page 190 & 191**	Chimp, white.....55.00
14" Beige Bear.....375.00	Child's Bear.....35.00	"Coco".....55.00
9" German Import.....200.00	Ideal Bear.....35.00	Steiff Cat on Wheels.....500.00
22" Cotton Plush Bear....55.00	"Gentle Ben".....55.00	Ichabod.....2,800.00
8" Wooly Plush Bear.....15.00	Knickerbocker Bears...ea 20.00	21½" German.....2,800.00
Picnic Bear.....200.00	"Petsy".....125.00	**Page 220 & 221**
Teddy Bear Pitcher.....15.00	**Page 192 & 193**	22" German Character.2,800.00
15" Standing Bear.....300.00	26" Steiff.....300.00	Unwigged Doll.....2,500.00
Page 176 & 177	12" "Cosy Teddy".....125.00	German Postal Carrier..2,500.00
14" Character Bear.....35.00	Hermann Cuddly Bear...115.00	**Page 222 & 223**
Bass.....20.00	7½" "Cosy Teddy".....75.00	Inspection Sargeant...2,500.00
18" Bassist.....225.00	**Page 194 & 195**	Steiff Girl.....850.00
Piano/stool.....55.00	"Cosy Orsi".....40.00	11" Girl & Boy Pair...1,500.00
Violin.....15.00	16" Wooden Bear.....20.00	Steiff Bird.....55.00
25" Pianist.....275.00	13" Synthetic Plush.....35.00	Steiff Beauty.....750.00
Drum.....150.00	"Bashful".....35.00	**Page 224 & 225**
17½" Drummer.....185.00	13" White Bear.....60.00	Leprechaun.....850.00
10" Gold Mohair.....225.00	Peggy Nisbet Bear.....85.00	11" Steiff Girl.....800.00
13" Steiff.....450.00	**Page 196 & 197**	Dog Pull Toy.....500.00
Page 178 & 179	Chan.....20.00	Tea Cosey.....850.00
18" Ideal Smokey.....45.00	Elizabeth Bear-et Browning.65.00	16" Steiff Doll.....450.00
18" No. 2 Smokey.....75.00	Amelia Bear-heart.....95.00	14" Steiff Doll.....750.00

Steiff "Lucki"..........200.00	"Floppy Cat & Cockie"...45.00	Leopard.............125.00
Squirrel Hand Puppet.....25.00	"Ginny's Pup".........150.00	5½" "Lion Cub".........55.00
Page 226	4" "Peky".............35.00	**Page 268 & 269**
"Mecki" & "Micki".......35.00	6" "Peky".............50.00	5" Lion Sitting.........45.00
Mecki Children.......ea. 30.00	**Page 250 & 251**	11" King Lion "Leo".....65.00
Panda...............150.00	"Hexie"..............40.00	4½" Lion Standing.......45.00
Page 228 & 229	Monkey..............95.00	"Lea".................55.00
Steiff Donkey.........700.00	"Waldi"..............150.00	Ideal Lion.............15.00
Steiff Camel..........700.00	Rabbit...............65.00	3" Elephant............85.00
Steiff Dachshund.......300.00	"Record Hansi"........175.00	8½" Elephant...........95.00
Elephant.............600.00	"Niki"...............175.00	"Cosy Trampy".........65.00
Monkey..............125.00	**Page 252 & 253**	**Page 270 & 271**
Pug Dog.............750.00	Rabbits............ea. 45.00	17" "Okapi"...........225.00
St. Bernard...........900.00	"Manni"..............125.00	6½" "Okapi"...........55.00
Page 230 & 231	11" "Begging Rabbit"...125.00	"Zebra"...............85.00
King "Leo"...........750.00	11½" Puppet...........45.00	Panther..............150.00
Zebra...............500.00	"Lamby"..............75.00	"Coco"...............55.00
Donkey..............550.00	Black Lamb...........85.00	**Page 272 & 273**
Buster Brown's Dog....300.00	"6½" Cow"............80.00	"Jocko"..............125.00
"Bully" dog..........250.00	"Floppy Lamb".........45.00	"Record Peter".........175.00
Page 232 & 233	Donkey..............175.00	"Elephant"............35.00
7" Mickey Mouse.......650.00	9½" Pull Toy Cow......295.00	"Bambi"..............35.00
5¼" Minnie Mouse......650.00	"Lamby"..............55.00	Plate................25.00
"Cockie".............45.00	Pink Felt Pig..........40.00	**Page 274 & 275**
4½" Mohair "Bully"...ea. 95.00	**Page 254 & 255**	"Bocky"..............65.00
Cottontail............135.00	"Lamby"..............45.00	"Perri"...............45.00
Page 234 & 235	"Floppy Lamby"........135.00	"Possy"..............45.00
Colt................125.00	"Baby Goat"...........65.00	"Xorry"..............45.00
Fox Terrier...........150.00	"Guinea Pig"..........25.00	"Cosy Fuzzy".........55.00
Polar Bears.......pr. 1,500.00	"Porcupine"...........35.00	"Cosy Zicky"..........55.00
Page 236 & 237	Goldfish.............165.00	**Page 276 & 277**
"Susi"..............135.00	Felix................65.00	"Mountain Lamb".......55.00
"Fluffy".............85.00	"Pony"...............45.00	10" "Nagy"...........175.00
Steiff Dog...........150.00	"Chimpanzee", brown....45.00	6½" "Nagy"...........85.00
Kitty...............110.00	"Chimpanzee", white....55.00	4" "Nagy"............45.00
Page 238	Pig.................55.00	"Raccy"..............45.00
Dog................135.00	**Page 256 & 257**	Porcupine............55.00
"Chow-Chow Brownie"...165.00	"Eric the Bat"........250.00	"Joggi"..............45.00
Page 240 & 241	Lion Cub.............15.00	**Page 278 & 279**
Steiff Ark............650.00	**Page 258 & 259**	"Murmy"..............55.00
Musical Cat..........300.00	Spider...............225.00	"Diggy"..............55.00
Sitting Siamese........150.00	"Crabby".............200.00	14" Seal.............85.00
"Mopsy".............75.00	"Gaty"...............150.00	"Slo".................35.00
"Lizzy"..............75.00	Elephant Head........300.00	**Page 280 & 281**
"Susi"..............55.00	**Page 260 & 261**	"Robby".............45.00
Page 242 & 243	"Kangoo"............250.00	"Paddy".............55.00
Mama "Kitty Cat".......85.00	"Moosy".............225.00	"Slo".................95.00
Kittens..............45.00	"Wild Boar"..........135.00	"Froggy"............35.00
6½" "Kitty Cat".......85.00	**Page 262 & 263**	"Pieps"..............30.00
4" "Kitty Cat".........75.00	"Bison"..............200.00	"Wittie".............35.00
"Topsy".............45.00	Dromedary Camel......200.00	**Page 282 & 283**
"Snurry"............135.00	17" Llama............225.00	Penguin.............95.00
5½" "Tabby".........75.00	11" Llama............85.00	"Goose".............65.00
4" "Tabby"..........45.00	6½" Llama...........65.00	Duck................55.00
3½" "Tabby".........45.00	**Page 264 & 265**	**Page 284 & 285**
17" Puss 'N Boots.....200.00	Fox.................450.00	"Cock" & ducks......ea 20.00
Page 244 & 245	13½" Tiger...........85.00	Chickens.............20.00
10" Puss 'N Boots.....150.00	28" Tiger............400.00	"Teddyli", "Bibbie", "Cocoli"
White Cat............25.00	22" Tiger............125.00	............ea 150.00
Black Cat............75.00	25" Tiger............350.00	Hide-A-Gift Bunnys.....ea 75.00
"Cosy Siam".........55.00	29" Tiger............350.00	**Page 286 & 287**
Page 246 & 247	7" Tiger, Japan, 7"....15.00	"Waldili".............225.00
"Molly".............95.00	9" Steiff Tiger........55.00	"Zipper Nauty".......125.00
"Foxy".............75.00	6" Steiff Tiger........45.00	"Jolly Cockie".......125.00
"Floppy Beagle"......55.00	Cubs & Rhino.......ea 45.00	**Page 288**
"Tessie"............125.00	**Page 266 & 267**	Hand Puppets.........25.00
Dalmatian...........250.00	"Leo"...............350.00	"Zebra"..............45.00
Copies of Pets......ea 50.00	"Lion Cub"...........85.00	
Page 248 & 249	Giraffe..............375.00	
"Snobby"...........35.00	45" King Lion "Leo"....600.00	
"Zotty".............150.00	16" "Lion Cub".......175.00	
"Cockie"............95.00	19" "Cub"...........400.00	

8

I.
Introduction

President Theodore Roosevelt

Teddy Bear enthusiasm is as strong today as at its birth in 1903. In that year Margarete Steiff in Germany and Morris Michtom, who later formed the *Ideal Novelty Co.* in America, crafted toy bears that were subsequently called "Teddy Bears". The undisputed fact is that the best loved toy of all time was named after Theodore Roosevelt, (President, 1901-1909).

Roosevelt was already the foremost field naturalist of his time, a hunter, rancher, explorer, soldier, prolific writer on diverse subjects, conservationist who did more for conservation than any American leader before or since, and, of course, politician and President. He was the first American to win the Nobel Peace Prize (for helping end the Russo-Japanese War); he busted trusts and built the Panama Canal. TR was not unlike a "Renaissance Man," (multi-talented), making him one of the most interesting Americans who ever lived, and, curiously, the father of the Teddy Bear.

Though Roosevelt recognized the magic of the real bear in its natural environment and its appeal to the public mind, he seems never to have spoken publicly about the Teddy Bear and gave the matter little attention. He, himself, never considered the animal a personal symbol and preferred the much less popular moose.* Nevertheless, on a hunting trip in Nov. 1902, President Teddy Roosevelt refused to shoot an old sick bear that had been tied to a tree by other hunters. The issue was immortalized by Clifford Berryman, a political cartoonist for the *Washington Post*, who used the incident to illustrate a boundary dispute, depicting the animal as a shivering little bear cub. How ironic that the worst hunt of Roosevelt's life forever linked his name to the elusive bear. One wonders if the Teddy Bear would have been the commercial success it is had it been named differently.

Conservation of Teddy Bears

The supply of early Teddy Bears is more limited than it appears. If the original models are to be extant in one hundred years, conservation techniques must be implemented now. Conservation refers to stabilizing the present condition and preventing further physical deterioration. Restoration refers to returning the item to its original appearance. Temperature and relative humidity are factors. Hygrometers are in continual use in the vault where the Smithsonian bear "lives" in his drawer at the National Museum of History and Technology. (See Illustration 1.).

---

*Schullery, Paul (ed.). *American Bears, Selections from the Writings of Theodore Roosevelt.* Colorado: Colorado Associated University Press, 1983.

Conservation problems arise due to the material out of which the toy is fabricated, textiles being the most difficult to conserve after paper. An early straw stuffed Teddy Bear is already in "guarded condition" because of the high acid content of straw. Furthermore, its textile covering becomes dry with age and tears with the slightest pressure. Dust, especially that from a polluted atmosphere, is acidic and abrasive and will wear its fur down.

To reduce these dangers, gently vacuum the bear through a net. Do not display in flourescent light or sunlight; use incandescent light bulbs (tungsten) which have no damaging ultra violet rays. Avoid high fluctuations in temperature. Exercise care in storage (keep away from water pipes). Make sure that there is no glue on the toy, as glue is a favorite nutrient of insects. Avoid metal pins which corrode. There are conservation concerns with display: without proper support the toy will sag in one direction.

If you must practice restoration in an attempt to improve the appearance of the Teddy Bear, use the "Reversible Theory;" anything that you do should be able to be removed harmlessly. For example, the recovering of a bear's pads can be undone. Finally, always wash your hands before handling an old stuffed toy.

Illustration 1. The Smithsonian Bear is one of the first models made by the *Ideal Novelty Co.* Note the vivid gold due to its conservation. The long snout, hump, long curved arms, big feet and oversize ears are evident. Photograph courtesy of the *Smithsonian's National Museum of History and Technology.*

Teddy Bears and Children

For the most part, it seems that children and Teddy Bears bond mainly for a reason long suspected but just now being examined. Teddy Bears are soothing creatures, attentive and sensitive to the owner's moods. Protective feelings expressed toward the Teddy Bears might be extended toward fellow humans. (See Illustration 2.).

The Teddy Bear fulfills basic needs that most of us have: to change the focus of attention away from ourselves, to touch and fondle. Even today in the collector's arena there are provocative and moving testaments to the deep emotional value of collecting Teddy Bears and toys.

The Teddy Bear age is most often considered to be from 5-11 years. It is not so much what the inanimate object is but what children for 75 years have bestowed upon it.

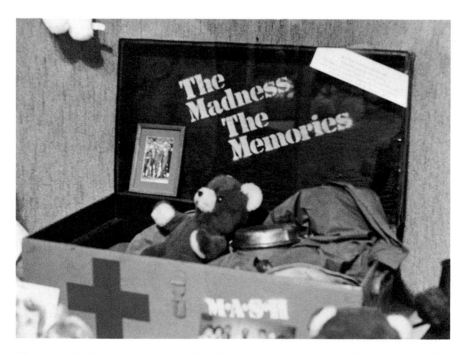

Illustration 2. The exact bear buried in this time capsule (army trunk) on the second to last segment of M-A-S-H. The actual Teddy Bear that was Radar's companion for over ten years has been retired. Photograph courtesy *20th Century-Fox* and *Denver Museum of Natural History*.

II.
Teddy Bear
Guidelines

Teddy Bear Guidelines, What to Look For

An appraisal takes into account a number of factors: condion, quality, rarity and desirability. In older bears this "desirability" is defined as: beauty of the old mohair in soft colors (black is a rare exception); straw stuffing (no attempt has been made in this book to differentiate between straw and excelsior); shoe button eyes which are set deeper than glass eyes and extend past glass in the time frame (plastic eyes have sharp outer edges); hump (by virtue of early construction techniques); long arms extending to the knees; paws slightly curved, tapering at the end; long feet (the length of feet to the height of bear is a ratio of 1:5); felt pads (oval or an elongated triangle); embroidered claws; triangular design of a smallish head forming a long pleasingly pointed snout; for those seeking Teddys before 1905, often there is a center head seam in the gusset between the ears and extending to the tip of nose; and finally, jointing at neck, shoulders and hips.

Most collectors concentrate on Teddy Bears before WW II. One way of dating is the "Sniff Test." Old straw can acquire a 1920's mustiness. Proper identification (and dating) is impossible from drawings in early trade magazines. Many bears in this book are from the original owner making exact dating possible.

Measure the bear without including the ears. An average price for a fine old light gold bear of good lineage is $350.00. One must add value for unusual size and/or condition; special appeal or other unique qualities such as color and mechanical performance. Slightly worn pads can be tolerated but most require excellent fur. Badly worn bears lose 50% of their value will add 10-25% to the value. The best goes up--the middle stays the same--the lowest goes down. Prices in this book are for *that* particular bear. Every effort has been made for a comprehensive representation of most all the genus and species of Teddy Bears known.

Price Guide Per Inch

(As a rule of thumb and based on fine condition)

Before 1912, black or dark brown mohair, Steiff/button. $50.00.
Before 1912, white curly or silky mohair, Steiff/button. $40.00-45.00.
Before 1912, pale gold mohair, Steiff/button. $30.00-35.00.
Before 1912, black mohair bear, not Steiff but fine quality. $35.00.
Before 1912, long pile light golden mohair, not Steiff but comparable quality. $25.00-28.00.
Before 1920, lt. golden mohair of lesser quality, but appealing (American). $16.00-19.00.
1915-1925, gold short pile or bristle mohair, often with twill nose (American). $12.00-17.00.
1920's luxurious white mohair, thicker feet. $15.00-20.00.
Brown bear on cast iron wheels. $16.00-22.00.
1920-30, cotton plush or mohair in colors (pink, red, green, etc.). $15.00-18.00.
1920-30, bright gold cotton plush, no claws. $12.00.
Schuco "Yes/No" Teddy Bears (various periods). $18.00-20.00.
1930's dark brown or gold mohair, embroidered or *metal* nose, rounder head, flatter snout (not inset). $10.00-14.00.
Made in England; circa 1930-50. $13.00.
Finest quality European import; circa 1950-60. $13.00-15.00.
Steiff "Zotty." $13.00.
Steiff "Cosy Teddy." $10.00.
Knickerbocker-type (inset snout), fully jointed; circa 1938. $6.00-8.00.
Knickerbocker-type (inset snout), fully jointed; circa 1958. $5.00.
Roly-Poly, stubby limbs, unjointed; circa 1950's-on. $2.50.
N.P.A. indicates "No Price Available."
C.S.P. indicates "Current Sales Price."

III.
Margarete
Steiff Co.,

DOLLS & ANIMALS

MARGARETE STEIFF CO.

TEL: . . . .

Dolls and
Animals

Margarete Steiff Gmbh Dolls and Animals

Steiff products appeal to everyone: children, naturalists, artists and collectors. Much of the art is self-recognizable. However, there is no proof-positive unless the toy has the famous "Button in Ear." It can nevertheless be "attributed" through documentation.

Although an invalid in her life, a talented Suabian girl from Giengen. Margarete Steiff, made a lasting contribution to the toy/doll world. The importance of this contribution is more and more apparent. Her dolls and toys with utmost artistic attention were innovative and original, as all art must be to endure. The dolls were revolutionary for their time, free from the sugary smartness and insipid "dollishness" of the average factory product. Due to their exceptional and large shoes, they were the first perfectly balanced, self supporting doll.

These remarkable dolls with felt heads and a seam down the middle were in production from 1894-1922. The earliest dolls did not have the button in ear. The original clothes were extraordinary and necessary for the value of the doll today. Designed with simplicity, the doll line included: Bavarian children; jovial lads; buxom maidens; university students; policemen; soldiers with equipment; farmers; are typified by good-natured exaggeration of features and posture and often comical expressions. (See Illustrations 3 and 4). These characters can be circus performers; mountebanks, clowns, wittily contrived German townspeople in the gay national costume; village musicians; village schoolmaster/children; Polish workingmen; Irish footmen; Chinese; American Indian; a Biliken-type; tea coseys and puppets; and marionettes with sarcastic caricature, designed by Albert Schlopsnies. Steiff has produced figures of fairy-tales and legends, and comic strip art, as well as window displays.

The success of the Teddy Bear greatly increased the sale of all the engaging stuffed aniamls. Today the Margarete Steiff Co. has four factories: two in West Germany (one of which is Giengen); one in Austria and one in Tunisia. They sell no

Illustration 3. Showing the amusing scene "At the Photographers." *International Studio,* January 1912.

16

toys to Communist countries and take pride in using only products from West Germany, Steiff models manufactured for West German consumption can be slightly different than those for export.

Illustration 4. "The Advertisement," suggesting the transfer of humor to an every day situation. *International Studio*, January 1912.

Steiff Guidelines, What to Look For

Stuffed animals have the closure with a *center* seam on the underside. How to measure: it is simplest to measure the greatest distance, i.e. vertical for sitting; horizontal for lying. Do not include the tail. However, the Steiff catalogues usually list the height only in their numbering system. Over the years different animals would be assigned the same catalog number. Furthermore, the same animal could be assigned different numbers. The last two digits before the comma *or* after the slash on the I.D. ear tag refer to the size in centimeters; for example, 5335,2 or 0202/36. ONLY the Steiff toys herein are reported in centimeters as well as inches because these are derived directly from the company's catalogues. However, the formula (2.54 cm./inch) shows mathematical discrepancies in the factory listings.

Absolutes of dating are to be avoided. A toy might be kept in the German warehouse for a period of years before reaching the shelf and then remain there more years. Changes in materials and symbols were gradual and could occur over a span of time. There are gaps in Steiff's records especially prior to WW II (this is often the case with toy and doll companies).

17

The issue of the blank ear button: it is found often enough on the early toys (and sometimes later ones) to require a reasonable assumption. These same blank clips were used for decorative buttons on clothes for dolls and monkeys. When the factory ran low of printed ones, these, of whatever metal alloy was available, were substituted. A blank button usually enhances the value. A pewter-type (dull grey) ear button with printing/ff underscored and prong-type attachment is older (pre WW II); but an old ear button is not always pewter color. It can be shiny. The manner of inscription overrides the alloy.

If you find a postwar toy with an ear I.D. tag, the catalog number with a comma is earlier than a slash which appeared in 1968. The post war products are so well marked that they can be described and sold over the telephone, a decided advantage when one is making an investment. Market trends indicate that collectors are demanding these definitive markings on toys, especially those of post WW II production. All of the prices listed in the Steiff section are based on mint condition; metal button in the ear; and paper chest tag, where applicable.

Chronology Table (Steiff)

Very early years: felt only, shoe button eyes
1903: mohair introduced.
1903: elephant symbol on paper tag attached to collar or bow.
1905: Steiff registered in Germany *Knopf im Ohr* (Button in Ear) trademark.
1905: voice box introduced.
1908: glass eyes introduced.
1905-1940: metal ear button (printing style/ff underscored, two prong attachment).
1907-1940: paper (chest) tag changed to blue bear with a watermelon mouth.
1915: velveteen introduced.
Before 1940: sheared rayon plush (velour) used.
1930's: *orange* I.D. ear tag.
1945-1972: blue bear's mouth on paper chest tag changed from watermelon to inverted "V".
1945-1972: shiny metal ear button with raised type resembling flowing handwriting, still PRONG attachment.
1950's: heyday of Steiff.
1950's: Dralon introduced.
1972--on: shiny ear button rivetted now, same flowing type, but incised.
1972--on: paper chest tag changed from yellow/red/blue bear to yellow/red circle.
1975-1978--on: change from mohair (exception bears) to synthetics.
1976-77--on: bear pads changed from felt to jersey knit.
1982--on: shiny silver button changed to gold color; still rivetted; same incised script; cloth I.D. tag replaces paper.

IV.
Miniature
Teddy Bears

Acrobatic Bear: 4½″ gold mohair, all straw, fully jointed, flips over a bar. German clockwork mechanism. Early 1900's. $300.00. Ferriswheel-type: pair of white mohair, all straw, fully jointed, sit on a pin activated by clockwork mechanism to revolve in a circle with music. Beautifully balanced. Rare and desirable early 1900's toy in original condition. Courtesy Virginia Lillard. $450.00. Tin plate with Roosevelt bears, $60.00.

Kewpie with Teddy Bear, 3¾″/10 cm. high, all bisque Kewpie with flocked bisque bear. Paper heart, "Kewpie Germany". Round label on back, "Copyright Rose O'Neill." Marked 46 and C in a circle on feet. Rare. Courtesy Susan Passarelli. NPA.

Miniature bears are particularly hard to judge as to age. Also, they can be confused with cats in this size. Hermann bears have ears closer together than Steiff bears. Top: 5″ current Hermann in antique outfit; rarer color, bright yellow current Hermann bear, antique button of Teddy Bear full figure ($10.00-15.00); 6″ brown rayon plush, molded ears, black bead eyes, red nose, high shoulders, older Japanese. $25.00-35.00. Front row: 3½″ Steiff, 1910, brown mohair, hat, all straw, brown floss embroidered nose/mouth, black bead eyes, long feet. Very rare. $125.00-150.00; white high shoulder made in Japan 1953, molded ears, plastic eyes, yellow flannel pads. (Childhood bear of owner). Current 3½″ white Steiff. All courtesy Hazel Mathews.

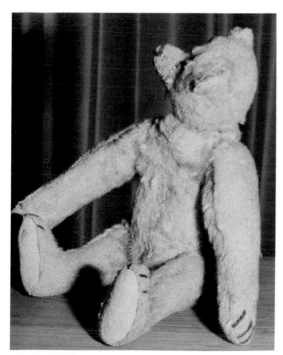

8″ beige mohair, all straw stuffed, deeply set shoe button eyes, long snout, floss nose and claws, long feet/triangular felt pads, no pads on arms which are markedly straight, fully jointed. Rare detail. Before 1920. Courtesy Marian Swartz. $175.00 up.

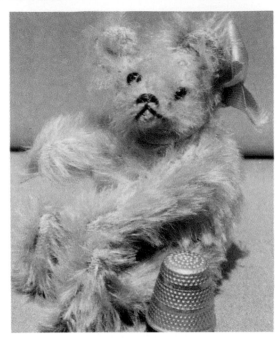

Steiff circa 1915: 3¾" white long pile mohair, all straw, fully jointed, black bead eyes, no pads, brown floss nose and mouth, curved back and big feet. A rare treasure for a miniaturist. Courtesy Wanda Loukides. $200.00-250.00.

Left: 5" Hermann circa 1920's. Reddish brown plush mohair, straw stuffed, fully jointed, tiny black shoe button-type eyes, no pads, black thread nose and mouth, long snout. $185.00. Grey metal cart made in Germany, $35.00. Right: 5" imported, 1940-50, bright gold mohair, straw stuffed, limbs wire jointed, rigid head, glass eyes/rod, no pads, black floss nose. $95.00 up. All courtesy Wanda Loukides.

Bathing Bear, 3″ mohair covered wire, bendable, black painted metal eyes, nose hard knotted thread, no pads. Unusual, circa: 1930-40. Courtesy Tammie Depew. $35.00-55.00.

Bear on pot metal wheels: 5½″ plush worn down to backing, straw stuffed, tiny plastic eyes, molded ears (Japan), plastic collar tacked on to bear. $25.00. Standing: 4″ honey mohair, straw stuffed, very long velveteen feet and snout (unusual), appealing expression. A choice miniature bear. Courtesy Marian Swartz. $75.00.

23

Unusual 3¾" beige mohair over metal Schuco Yes/No bear with two faces, circa 1955. Fully jointed, bear wags head when metal rod is rotated. Shows normal teddy face with metal eyes, floss nose and mouth. Front view shows "funny face" with metal eyes, nose and mouth with detailed tongue. Back view showing profile of faces and metal rod between legs. Courtesy of Janet Orashan. $150.00 up.

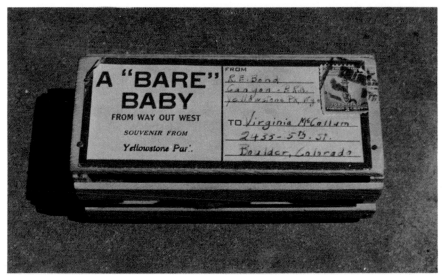

Clown from Japan: 5½″, white sheared rayon plush head, push down/spring encased squeaker toy. Glass eyes, embroidered nose. 1940's. $15.00.
5″ yellow high shoulder bear from Japan. Sold to tourists in crate as a souvenir from Yellowstone National Park. Pre World War II. Rare to find never out of box. $75.00.
Pink standing bear, 4¼″, high quality rayon plush covered plaster, glass eyes, made in Germany pre World War II. $35.00 up. All courtesy Diane Hoffman.

Postcard: "Every where that Mary went the bear was sure to go", Ullman Mfg. Co. 1907. $8.00. German wind-up, spins, 5½" flocked rayon plush, glass eyes, molded ears, paper mache legs, pin jointed arms, original clothes, 1950's. $35.00. Glass teddy bear Christmas ornament, 3", made in Western Germany, 1970's. $6.00. "Two's Company Three's none", copyright 1907, M.T. Sheahan, Boston (hard to find), $10.00. Teddy 2½" molded hollow rubber on plastic base, turn crank and bear moves. Interesting animation. $25.00. "Teddy" Bear Post Card Series I copyright 1906, Albert G. Reid, Boston, Mass. $8.00. Courtesy Diane Hoffman.

Teddy Bear School: 6 students with desks and 1 teacher. Made in Japan using the yellow high shoulder bears. Shackman reissued this boxed set in the 1970's. It was discontinued in 1980. This is the original version, missing apple on teacher's desk, blackboard and books. A classic. Courtesy Randi Parker. $35.00-45.00.

On the issue of High Shoulder and similar Japanese mini bears: all have rigid heads; 3-4½" size made in 1930-60 of wood with glued to body rayon sheered plush or cotton with a nap: flannel pads glued on: molded ears; the 3" size has limbs pin jointed to the outside similar to the all bisque dolls of the 1920-30's. The 4½" bear has metal loops on the inside of limbs to be strung with elastic or string. All have "stalk" eyes. The noses are also on a stem. These bears once flooded the market and many collectors of today played with them. There is some demand. Courtesy Susan Roeder. $25.00-35.00.

Left: 6½" Steiff circa 1930-40, short gold mohair, all straw, fully jtd., glass eyes, felt pads feet only, floss nose, mouth and claws, squeaker (unusual for a small bear). $185.00. Center: 5½" Steiff, beige mohair (one of the popular 1950's Steiff colors), hard stuffed straw, fully jointed, glass eyes, no pads, brown floss nose and mouth, long snout and long feet turn up. $125.00-150.00 up. Right: 6" Steiff, linen thread only on chest, gold mohair, original pale orange ribbon (woven edges), straw stuffed, fully jointed, glass eyes, no pads, black floss nose and mouth. Circa 1950. All courtesy Wanda Loukides.

Walking keywind bear on all fours: 6″ glass eyes. Japan 1950's. $25.00. Two-tone rayon plush, 6″, all straw, *blue* glass eyes, ears sliced in (often to be pulled out by abuse), unjointed. Cloth tag sewn in side seam, "Occupied Japan." Circa 1945-52. These were produced as dashboard ornaments. Colorful. Courtesy Marian Swartz. $15.00.

Rare, older, snow white miniature Steiff, 4″, mohair, all straw, fully jointed, distinctive amber glass eyes, no pads, black floss nose and mouth. Large ears add to expression. Nicely shaped and detailed for such a small bear. Late 1940's, cloth tag sewn into left arm seam, "U.S. Zone Germany". Courtesy Wanda Loukides. $200.00-250.00.

Left: Steiff, 3½″, pewter ear button/ff underscored (pre World War II production), gold mohair, all straw, fully jointed, tiny black shoebutton-type eyes, no pads, black floss nose and mouth, long feet. Note how high ear button is placed. It is difficult to find a 3½″ Steiff with button because easily dislodged. $125.00. Right: Steiff 3½″, beige mohair, all straw, fully jointed, black bead eyes, no pads, brown floss nose and mouth, long feet. Note how variety in noses and mouths and pupillary distance changes expression. $100.00-125.00. All courtesy Wanda Loukides.

"Jackie," 6½″, Steiff's 50 year Jubilee Teddy (1953), golden mohair, all straw, fully jointed, glass eyes, felt pads on short legs. Brown floss embroidered mouth and nose with large white stitch, definitive of this sought after Teddy. Floss claws, longish snout, squeaker. Tiny little important bear. Courtesy Susan Passarelli. $450.00 up.

Hermann Bears (not to be confused with Steiff Bears), 5¾", white and brown mohair, tightly stuffed, plastic eyes, floss nose and mouth. Well attired. Circa 1958. Courtesy Carol Simons. $75.00 each.

Standing, 6", unusual dark brown mohair, all straw, fully jointed, brown glass eyes, black floss nose and mouth, prong-type ear button. Purchased in West Germany in 1965 for $1.00. Now $150.00. Standing "Young Bear," 5"/12cm., Steiff No. 12a/1312.0, caramel mohair, all straw, brown glass eyes, jointed head, felt pads, air brushed claws. The snout is shaved in the two larger sizes. Circa 1965. Courtesy Bev Murray. $75.00 up.

Key wind: 6″ walks, googly eyes, metal feet and hands. Called "The Graduate". 1959 example. $35.00. 6½″ key wind "Drummer", glass eyes, felt soles, beats drum and turns head. Courtesy Marian Swartz. Earlier, $35.00.

Petz Bear: 1940-50 7″, button on chest, brown/gold shaggy mohair, rubber face and ears, straw stuffed, eyes and nose painted black, flesh color felt hands/stitched fingers, same felt on feet/cardboard innersoles, embroidered claws on feet, tail. Darling shaped body, open mouth gives look of amazement. German. $95.00. Wooden swing, $15.00; glass bottle has Teddy Bear impression in mold, rubber nipple (marked Japan). Courtesy Nan C. Moorehead. $10.00.

31

"Hurry, you know that I can't hold this pose for long," says this 3½" Stieff Teddy. Beige mohair, fully jointed, straw stuffed, black bead eyes, long feet with no pads. Note the especially cute expression. Circa 1950. This is one of the best quality small bears ever made. Courtesy Deborah Ritchey. $100.00-125.00.

White mohair, Steiff, 3¼", all straw, black bead eyes, brown floss nose and mouth, fully jointed, long feet, thread where Steiff chest tag was. Rare white 1950's example. White reissued unjointed in 1982. $100.00-125.00. Beige mohair, 3½", same as above, well contoured tummy. Circa 1957 No. 12/5310. Courtesy Nancy Roeder. $75.00-100.00.

"Teddy" 6"/15cm. the original Teddy Bear, created by Steiff in 1903. Fully jointed, gold and beige (beige described as honey after 1978) mohair, long feet, glass eyes, chest tag thread, no ear clip, circa 1957. Original woven edge rayon ribbons, black floss noses, appealing size. No. 12/5315. Courtesy Nancy Roeder. $125.00 up.

Less than two pennies high: 1-3/8", brown vinyl unjointed bear. Post Cereals premium in 1969. Came with Storykin Goldilocks, a table, three bowls, three chairs and a bear. Chosen for his size and light weight, he has accompanied his owner on summit climbs of all 53 peaks in Colorado over 14,000 ft. Hard to find advertising miniature. Courtesy Carolyn Altfather. $10.00.

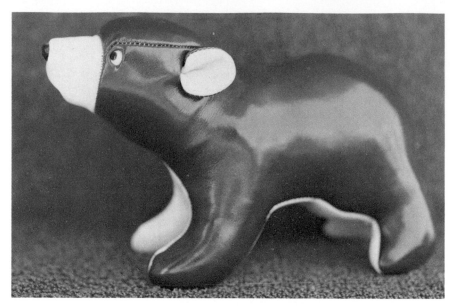

Oil cloth bear, standing, 4 1/8″, plastic nose and eyes, oilcloth tongue, hardstuffed. Commercially made, circa 1960. Courtesy Janet Orashan. $20.00.

Steiff "Tabby", 3¼″ 1950's. Played with so $25.00. Courtesy Cathy Darden. Right: honey color mohair bear, 7½″, straw head, cotton stuffed body, brown glass eyes, floss nose, jointed at neck only. Sits by bending wire in leg. Excellent quality from "Mutzli" Switzerland. Courtesy Nancy Schroeder. $45.00.

Snap Bear, 4 3/8″, made in China; corduroy, poly fiber stuffing, plastic eyes, embroidered features. Novelty: limbs snap on and off, destined to become rare due to loss of limbs. Courtesy Carol Simons. Cost $2.00 in 1983.

Peddler's Tray (See page 36 for information)

A peddler's tray is a popular way to display miniature Teddies. Peddler doll made by Nancy Burges: bisque doll, 14″, $125.00. 37 bears ranging in size from ¾″ to 4½″, price range $1.00-40.00. They are made of: porcelain, felt, velour, mohair, fur fabric, wood, plastic and flocking. Large white porcelain on bottom left is an original by Elizabeth Willis, $40.00. In basket lower left, light tan/blue ribbon, ltd. edition by Sylvia Lyons, $35.00; porcelain brown bear on red wheeled platform, center bottom, made by Mabel Oliphant, $15.00; white felt "Beararina" made by owner, $18.00; pinned to right side of cape is Tiggywinkle's "Ralph Rider" $35.00; top right of basket, mohair, fully jointed, older, $38.00. Courtesy Evelyn Thomas. Total of bears: $515.00.

V.
Teddy Bears
Before 1940

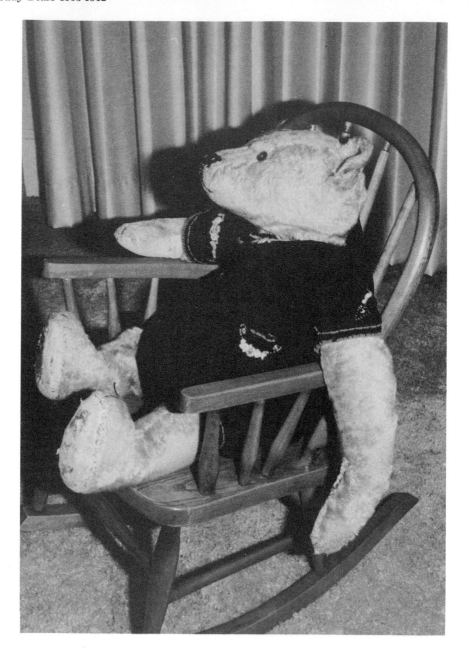

28″ silky white mohair showing very little wear, head and limbs straw stuffed, torso straw and kapok (soft for child to cuddle face), humpback, pearl buttons replace eyes, long feet, very long curved arms, triangular head, floss nose and claws, replaced canvas pads, fully jointed. Resembles the 1903 Steiff bear. Large size of any model can change appearance. This is an extraordinary bear, an armful for a child or collector. Courtesy Marian Swartz. $900.00 up.

Wish inspiring bear: 25" tall, long pile curly white mohair, all straw stuffed, large hard leather shoe button eyes, tan twisted floss embroidered nose, mouth and claws, pinkish tan pads of beaver felt, 5½" long feet, blank Steiff ear button. Early Steiff button enhances the value of this magnificent Teddy Bear. A significant addition to the serious collector at any price. Family bear from 1906-07. Courtesy Shirlee Glass. $1,100.00 up.

A king of stuffed toys: 16", long pile silky blonde mohair, straw stuffed, with kapok and straw in torso so that child could cuddle face. Original black shoe button eyes, rose twisted floss embroidered nose, mouth and claws, long feet, original felt pads, hump and long curved arms. In factory-new condition from 1903-05. Steiff characteristics. Courtesy Irma Leaver, original owner. $650.00 up.

One of the most sought after: 13" Steiff, blank pewter ear button (1903-05), light gold long pile thick mohair, straw stuffed, fully jointed, black shoe button eyes, coarse brown thread nose and mouth, and claws, beige felt pads, hump, long skinny feet, long curved arms, long snout. This exceptional condition attests to the durability of the Steiff product. $500.00-600.00 up. "Mother Goose's Teddy Bears," by Frederick L. Cavally, Jr., published in 1907 by The Bobbs-Merrill Co. with 32 full page color illustrations. Sadly, the original color prints are often torn out to be sold for $10.00 each. Considered rare in fine condition. All courtesy Wanda Loukides. $250.00.

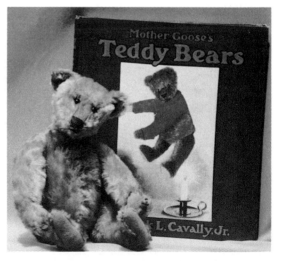

Example of all that collectors consider important: 16", light gold long pile silky mohair, all straw stuffed, deep set shoe button eyes, long snout on small head, dark brown floss nose, mouth and 4 claws, long curved arms, long feet with oval felt pads, and wine color wool innersoles; fully jointed. Minute differences of the first Teddy Bears, scarcely perceptible, gives a certain individuality. A classic from 1904-05. (Author). $650.00. Note the center head seam in gusset - adds value. This is found on some of the earliest Steiff Teddys (1903-05), after which time the pattern was changed.

"Emerson" is a wise and half-human bear, 20" light golden long pile silky mohair, all straw (Steiff did not stuff their bears as firmly as some companies), fully jointed with early blank ear button. Black shoe button eyes, brown embroidered nose, mouth and claws, long curved arms, light gold felt pads and large feet, acute hump. Circa before 1907. Value increases linearly with size. Whether 1903 or 1907 is immaterial and impossible to know. A treasure in any case. Courtesy Marlene Wendt. $750.00 up in magnificent condition.

Steiff bear with button: 8", early gold mohair, all straw, fully jointed, original shoe button eyes, black embroidered nose, mouth and claws, felt pads. Gentle sagging of the straw gives added charm. Even in this small example Steiff uses paws slightly curved tapering at the end. Original to bear; red/white polka dot cotton overalls, one of the various outfits inspired by Seymour Eaton's "The Roosevelt Bears, Their Travels and Adventures" marketed for bears soon after 1906. Posed in front of a wall hanging made of old college football cigarette silks. NPA.

20" Steiff with early ear button, mohair, all straw, jointed, flat 3/8" diam. hard leather shoe button eyes, rose floss nose, mouth and 4 claws, long curved arms, long snout and feet (4½"), beaver felt pads. The inside of ears and seams reveal that bear was originally off-white. The nose is embroidered with vertical stitches. After cleaning this very light golden color is achieved, albeit some collectors prefer the 1905 white bears in "found condition." Only a silk (not rayon or synthetic) bow is appropriate for this vintage. (Author). $800.00.

Rare dark brown Steiff, 13" mohair, straw stuffed, fully jointed, early ear button, black shoe button eyes, black floss nose, mouth and claws (4 threads), long arms (7"), dark gold felt pads, long feet (3"), long slender snout, squeaker. This color is much harder to find than white. Circa 1905. Named "Penny" because he came from Pennsylvania.
Book: *The Little Brown Bear* by Johnny Gruelle of Raggedy Ann and Andy fame. Dates 1920. Courtesy Marlene Wendt. Bear $375.00-475.00. Book $65.00.

1905 light golden mohair subdued with time: 14″, black shoe button eyes, brown embroidered nose, mouth and claws, long feet with felt pads, fully jointed. The fine expression of this bear suggests Steiff. Well dressed in antique setting. Courtesy Shirlee Glass. $350.00 up.

Bear of many distinctions: 12″ light gold long pile mohair, straw stuffed, fully jointed, glass eyes, broadly embroidered black nose, mouth and claws, tan felt pads, long feet and arms, long snout, large hump, press from *sides* and squeaker works (unusual). A perfectly proportioned 1907 bear. Trimmed with bells around his neck. Courtesy Marlene Wendt. $350.00 up.

44

Folk Art: a fascinating example of American Folk Art in an all cloth bear. An individually handstitched and conceived personality. 14″ brown double flannel (blanket), mattress buttons for eyes, pink embroidered nose and stitched claw decoration, stuffed with rags. Jointing is by bone buttons as on Dr. Denton sleepers. Circa 1910. Courtesy Hazel Mathews. $175.00.

One of the many manufacturers of quality bears before 1910: 13″, pale gold mohair, straw stuffed, fully jointed, black shiny shoe button eyes, black floss nose, mouth and claws (3 threads), long arms (6″), felt pads, long feet (2¾″), hump squeaker. Note ears set low on head. Riding his own papier mache horse. Innocent expression. Courtesy Marlene Wendt. $350.00 up.

1907 Steiff, 12″ light gold mohair, all straw, fully jointed, shoe button eyes, floss nose, mouth and claws, felt pads, long feet and arms, hump, squeaker. This expressive bear is unrestored and a great pride to owner Sarah McClellan. $400.00 up.

One of the first: 12″ rich gold mohair, all straw, fully jointed, deep set original shoe button eyes, floss nose, mouth and claws, beige felt pads, long feet/triangular pads, triangular head, long snout and acute hump. Shoulders are set high on torso to accentuate his long curved arms. This irresistible bear has had 25 sudsing/dunking baths in his life. This seems to have kept the mohair pile vibrant and fresh as though new, and attests to the excellent quality of the toy. A popular cabinet size to be put in the glass case it deserves. From original owner born in 1897, given bear when 6-7 years old when every child in America between the ages of 5-11 had a Teddy Bear on their wish list. Courtesy Ruby B. Wilson. $400.00.

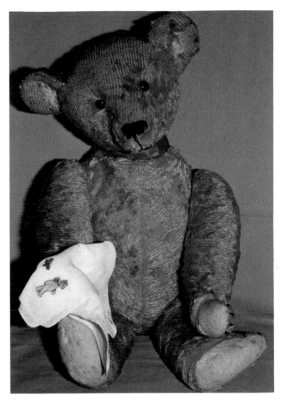

Most closely resembles the Smithsonian Bear, 21″ gold mohair, mixed cotton and straw stuffed, fully jointed, (head reattached), small glass eyes, black yarn embroidered nose, mouth and claws, felt pads on long slender hands and feet, long and slender snout, hump. Carries a hankie embroidered with a teddy bear. His expression is benign and paternal. Although worn, this T.R. portrait-type has a unique presence. Courtesy Margaret M. Carlson. $400.00.

Steiff, button in ear: 13″, light blonde long pile mohair, all straw stuffed, fully jointed with cardboard discs, black shoe button eyes, rust color floss nose, mouth and claws, long arms, felt pads on long feet, hump, squeaker. Note that ears are set far apart. A most engaging Teddy Bear, circa 1905. Courtesy Evelyn Krause. $450.00-up.

Steiff with pewter ear button, ff underscored: 12″ light gold mohair, straw stuffed, shoe button eyes, dark brown embroidered nose and claws, long snout on small head, long oval felt pads on long feet, long curved arms, fully jointed. A pre-1910 bear with Steiff pedigree. Courtesy Susan Buckman. $300.00 if nose reworked to original condition.

Steiff with "rusty" early ear button: 13″, desirable light gold curly mohair, straw stuffed, fully jointed, original shoe button eyes. The mouth treatment coincidentally resembles the early Steiff paper chest tag, (blue bear's head with watermelon mouth). It would seem that this favorite ancient bear has many happy stories to tell. Wearing antique Cal-Berkeley necktie; posed in front of original Bessie Pease Guttman print. NPA.

Favorite: 14", pale gold long pile mohair, original deep set shoe button eyes. (Many times owners replace glass eyes with old shoe buttons, both as a convenience and as a selling device. Look for a deep set quality.) All straw, black floss nose, mouth and claws, arms extending to knees, long feet and snout. A charming settling of the straw, a product which loses strength with time. Circa 1905. (Author). $350.00 up.

A honey of a Teddy Bear, 12", honey gold silky mohair, straw stuffed, fully jointed, long snout, shoe button eyes, black floss broad nose, floss mouth and claws, beige felt pads, long feet. Courtesy Wanda Loukides. $450.00 up.

16″ brown/gold longer mohair, all straw stuffed, black shoe button eyes, black embroidered nose and claws, original felt pads, long feet and markedly curved arms. Unusual ear treatment and hard to find color. This bear is more rare than a Steiff of the same early period. An unforgettable bear. Courtesy Marian Swartz. $350.00 up.

ne of the first Steiffs: 12″, gold ohair, all straw, fully jointed, iginal shoe button eyes, tan felt pads, black embroidered nose, mouth and claws, exported prior to the addition of voice boxes, long feet with triangular pads, long curved arms, long snout and hump, just enough settling of the straw to add charm. Wearing the mother of pearl purse purchased at same time as bear at a Fair in Nebraska. Courtesy Nancy Catlin. $400.00.

Hard-to-find early 11″ Teddy, long pile snow white mohair: popular child size, all straw, fully jointed, deep set shoe button eyes, triangular head, dark brown embroidered nose and mouth, no claws, leather-like fabric pads. Clothes are original to bear. His broad torso lends character. Given to Max Yeamans in 1905. Since his childhood days the bear has been in a cedar chest. It does not fit into any one category of manufacturer. Courtesy Vanita Y. French. $350.00 up.

A great old Teddy Bear attributed to Steiff: 19″, beige long pile silky mohair, all straw, hard leather shoe button eyes, black floss embroidered nose, mouth and claws, long snout, hump, felt pads on long feet, growler. This benign bear wins your heart. Courtesy Evelyn Krause. $500.00.

Collection of Teddy Bears and Dolls in owner's 1932 wicker stroller. (Author).

14″ gold mohair, all straw, original shoe button eyes, black floss nose and claws, hump, long snout, felt pads, long feet and arms. Unusually long torso, short legs and well contoured haunches. Probably American. Circa before 1910. Courtesy Teddy Fonseca. $350.00 up.

55

"Lucky," is 10", gold mohair, straw stuffed, fully jointed, glass eyes, floss nose, mouth and claws with large stitches, acute hump, long arms and feet, felt pads. He has a great deal of "class" for a bear his size. An unusual look to add variety to a collection. Circa before 1908. Courtesy Roberta Viscusi. $450.00.

Steiff with blank button: 14″ honey color early mohair, all straw with kapok in torso, black shoe button eyes, black floss nose, mouth and claws, hump, squeaker, fully jointed. Before 1910. Courtesy Diane Hoffman. In this pristine condition $450.00 up.

Top: "Twins," 14" scant gold mohair, straw stuffed, fully jointed, shoe button eyes, black floss nose and claws, squeaker, original leather pads which suggest early French origin. Classics before 1910 are hard to find. Courtesy Beverly L. Krein. $500.00 pair in this condition.

"Laughing Roosevelt Bear," made by The Columbia Teddy Bear Mfrs. 17" rust mohair, all straw, fully jointed, shoe button eyes, pointy felt pads. To open and close the mouth, just press bears tummy or turn head which activates spring mechanism. He grins from "ear-to-ear" showing his two white milk glass teeth. Others are painted. This bear would be hard to replace. Courtesy Helen Sieverling. $500.00 up.

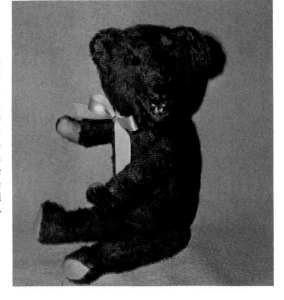

15″ sparse bristle mohair, all straw, ears sliced into head, pin wire jointing replaced eyes, open flannel-felt mouth with tongue, yarn nose and claws. Japan 1920-30. Unusual and likeable. Courtesy V.M. Davis. $75.00.

Early 14″ bear with triangular head: gold mohair, all straw, fully jointed. The loved condition emphasizes his shoe button eyes. Remains of embroidered floss nose, claws, felt pads on 2½″ long feet (not shown). Large ears set high on head, better to listen to the child's confidences. No voice box. American. Dating: exactly 1908, from original owner, Ernest H. Schroeder. Of great sentimental value. In this condition, because of age, $195.00.

Steiff: 10″, cream color long pile mohair, straw stuffed, shoe button eyes, embroidered rust color nose, mouth and claws, long arms, hump and big feet. Typical Steiff appearance. The stuffing and fur gives him a "real bear" look. Circa 1904-05. Courtesy Roberta Viscusi. $450.00 up.

Perfect size for 22″ doll; 10″ white long pile mohair, straw stuffed, torso kapok/straw, shoe button eyes, brown floss nose and claws, felt pads, long feet and hump. No ear button but suggests Steiff circa: 1905. Courtesy Diane Hoffman. In this pristine condition $450.00.

"Louie" so named because he came from a doll convention in St. Louis, 17" Steiff, before 1910 lustrous soft gold mohair, all straw, fully jointed, black shoe button eyes, brown embroidered nose, mouth and claws, acute hump, long snout, long curved arms and feet. His original felt pads were expertly recovered long ago and do not affect the value of this "Favorite Bear." The blue denim vest was added and is autographed by Hans Otto Steiff and other well known bear celebrities. Courtesy Marlene Wendt. $475.00 up, and will continue to rise.

Low shouldered bear giving long neck appearance: 15" light golden mohair, all straw stuffed, fully jointed, original shoe button eyes, broadly embroidered dark brown floss nose, floss mouth and claws. Ears suggestive of Ideal Novelty Co. circa 1906-07. Courtesy Marlene Wendt. $400.00 up.

61

Steiff bear with ear button: 9″, honey long pile mohair, straw stuffed, fully jointed, shoe button eyes deeply set, dark brown floss nose, mouth and claws, long snout, acute hump, felt pads, long feet and curved arms. Wonderful Teddy Bear detail in this small size. Dates exactly 1905 from original owner, Violet E. Duncan. $300.00 up with ear button.

English Bear: 13″, caramel mohair, straw stuffed, fully jointed, shoe button eyes, brown floss nose, mouth and claws, felt pads, long feet, long curved arms and long snout, acute hump. Note that the appearance is different from the German or American bears of this period. Original owner born in England in 1908. A fine early bear that has kept his dignity. Courtesy Dorothy R. Jones. $350.00 up.

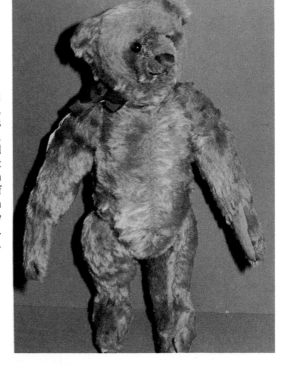

Exact dating from original owner, 1910, Steiff with ear button, 12″ light golden mohair, straw stuffed, fully jointed, shoe button eyes, felt pads replaced, floss nose, mouth and claws, squeaker, hump. A great similarity to the bears in "Mother Goose's Teddy Bears." Courtesy Ruth L. Ruder $400.00 up.

Ruth L. Ruder shown on first birthday with "Teddy" who frightened her at first, but by the time the picture was taken she was willing for him to be near her.

"Woodberry" and "Teddy", unplayed with and played with, Margaret Strong bears, 10"
size, light brown mohair, stuffed with foam rubber and cotton (has begun to sag in bear
on right), fully jointed, hump back (more pronounced after play), voice box, felt pads (a
few holes requiring Band-aids). Bear on right is a dead-ringer for the bear Margaret Strong
played with in 1904. Also, for the "First Birthday" Teddy Bear shown on page 63. Courtesy
Carolyn and Elizabeth Mathews.

Left: 9½" mohair, straw, sawdust
and kapok, shoe button eyes, floss
nose, long snout, triangular felt
pads, very long feet and arms, fully
jointed. Probably German, suggestive of Steiff. 1908 from
original owner. $200.00.
Diminutive friend: sweet 8", gold
mohair, straw stuffed, shoe button
eyes, long snout, embroidered
nose worn, replaced pads, long
feet. Petite early American bears
are hard to find. Easily lost or
discarded. 1908 from original
owner. Courtesy Mary Ann Bonnell. $200.00 up.

Impish: 12″ long pile pale gold mohair, straw head and limbs, straw and kapok torso, black shoe button eyes, triangular head, hump, black embroidered nose (mouth missing) and claws, long curved arms set low on torso, oval felt footpads on long feet. Comes with provenance: purported to be one of those teddy bears disributed to chosen children from the observation platform of Teddy Roosevelt's campaign train in Huron, SD. $350.00-400.00. Farm wagon, 16″, lithographed wooden horse and wagon on cast iron wheels circa 1910. $95.00-125.00. All courtesy Nancy Nelson. Cow, horse and pig, 5½″, flocked paper mache, German circa 1910, $25.00 each; 3½″ wind up rooster, velvet and felt $35.00.

Madonna: mother, 16″ long pile blonde mohair, all straw, clear glass eyes with dark pupil, umber stitched nose and claws, long snout, pink felt pads, cardboard innersoles, long feet and arms. This Teddy Bear can make a collector addictive. $450.00 up. Child: 8″ beige mohair, all straw, original shoe button eyes, black stitched nose and claws, felt pads (feet only), fully jointed. It is reasonable to assume an early Steiff. $200.00. Both courtesy Beverly L. Krein.

65

Teddy Bear that enjoys sitting in his wicker buggy: 21″ long pile golden mohair, straw stuffed, fully jointed, glass eyes, floss nose, mouth and claws, hump, growler hidden inside (not discernible because of bear's large size), long arms (10½″), felt pads on long feet (4″). Courtesy Marlene Wendt. $600.00 up.

Silky light cream mohair, 22″, all straw, fully jointed, shoe button eyes, tannish pink floss nose, mouth and claws, pads appear replaced on long feet, (color of pads should blend with fur covering), long curved arms, long snout and hump. Note shoulders are set low. Superior materials and workmanship on this close relative of a Steiff. One must guard against casual attribution of bears to various factories without solid basis in fact or comparison. Finding a bear like this is one of the rewards of collecting. Circa, before 1910. Courtesy Stacie Flaners. $600.00 up.

Burnished gold mohair, 12″, all straw, original shoe button eyes dark brown floss nose, mouth and claws, felt pads, no squeaker. Steiff button has slipped *inside* of ear. A dead ringer for the currently available Margaret Strong Bear. 9″ muslin doll, hard stuffed, factory joined from printed sheets. From dress style, circa 1920. Courtesy Hazel Mathews. Bear $400.00-450.00; Doll $45.00.

16″ light gold mohair mellowed to beige, all straw with torso hard and unyielding in contrast to his soft outer covering, shoe button eyes, with glasses ($8.00-10.00), floss nose, mouth and claws, long snout, *beaver* felt pads with cardboard innersoles, slender ankles. Highest quality, circa 1912. $400.00 up. Stereoptican viewer, tin, 25 animal view cards. Courtesy Hazel Mathews. $125.00.

Grover Cleveland, named for that street in St. Paul, MN from whence he came, 12", baby fine woolly mohair, hard stuffed straw, fully jointed, glass eyes, black embroidered nose, mouth and claws, 5 thread, felt pads. Some of his exaggerated characteristics to make him a "keeper;" unusual shape body, huge hump, long arms (6½"), big feet (2½"), squeaker activated by pressing *sides* of body, long snout and oversize ears giving him a unique expression. Red knit sweater is original to bear. Before 1910. Courtesy Marlene Wendt. 25% added for white, $350.00-400.00.

Teddy Bear with same nose treatment that is often found on Steiff animals: 13″, curly pale golden mohair, all straw, fully jointed, original shoe button eyes, long snout, black embroidered nose, mouth and claws, long curved arms, acute hump, long feet, squeeze voice box. Every person needs at least one of this type! Courtesy Virginia Joy. circa 1910. $350.00-400.00 up.

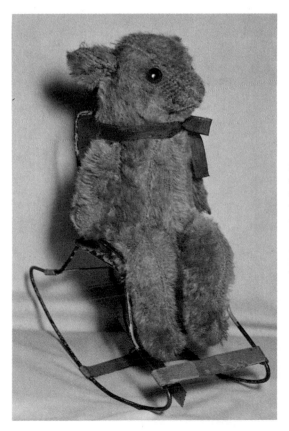

Bear in rocker: 9½″, cinnamon mohair, straw stuffed head, glass eyes. Bear's lower body is formed over a metal cannister attached to the base of a blue painted metal chair. Primitive mechanism. Early mechanicals are scarce. These life-like performing bears compliment a collection, *IF* you can find them. NPA.

Steiff, 12", pewter ear button/ff underscored, pale gold mohair, straw stuffed, fully jointed, brown glass eyes/black pupils, beige pads with black thread claws, black floss nose and mouth, squeaker. Hump on back, big feet and extra long curved arms. Circa 1910. Courtesy Wanda Loukides. $450.00-500.00 up.

Long armed bear: 12", long pile white mohair, straw stuffed, kapok/straw torso, orange claws and mouth (minus nose embroidery), long snout, squeaker, felt pads. Personality plus! A most unique bear to treasure. Add value for white color and excellent condition. Courtesy Kayleen Peterson. $350.00 up.

14″, Minerva, all metal shoulderhead. Marks: "Minerva" across front. "Germany/3" on back. This style is circa 1915. Rare royal blue plush Teddy Bear body, straw stuffed, fully jointed, felt pads. Courtesy Kay Bransky. $250.00-300.00 up.

Bear Boy, 11½″, celluloid molded/painted face, brown wool plush suit, felt mitts and boots, straw stuffed, jointed at shoulders and hips with wire, circa 1910-20 in answer to the Teddy Bear Boom. $110.00. Fur Bear Boy, 6″ attributed to Cuno & Otto Dressel, bisque head, painted blue eyes, five piece compo body, white fur suit/blue collar, $95.00. Tin key wind horse/cart. $35.00. All courtesy Nan C. Moorhead.

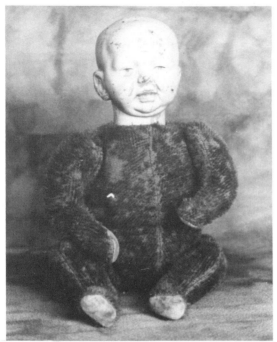

12″, Horsman *Baby Bumps Can't Break 'Em,* flange neck with red plush Teddy Bear body, straw stuffed. Created to the design of the cloth body. Head is unmarked. Circa 1912. These "Teddy Dolls" never became the rage as hoped and had a short production period. Very few *original* examples with a composition head can be found. Courtesy Kay Bransky. $350.00 up.

13″ early light gold mohair, all straw, fully jointed, glass eyes, black embroidered nose and claws, original felt pads, long feet and long curved arms and hump. Some wear to snout which is the most vulnerable to child's love. Perhaps this is why some much later bears are manufactured with shaved snouts. This one: circa 1910. Courtesy Wanda Vessels. $400.00.

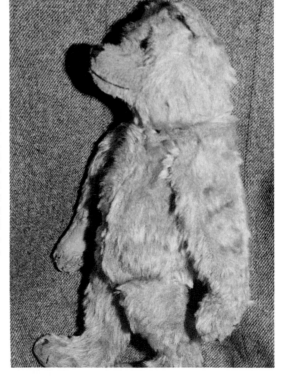

Protective Bear: 14″ long pile light gold mohair, all straw, floss nose, mouth and claws, one original glass eye, markedly curved forearms, long snout and hump. American. Circa 1910-15. Courtesy Hazel Mathews. $350.00 up.

Long silky light gold mohair, 18″, straw stuffed, fully jointed, floss nose, mouth, no claws, glass eyes, acute hump, long snout, triangular head, long curved arms, long feet with felt pads. Large size in beautiful condition. Circa 1910-15. Courtesy Vera Tiger. $400.00 up.

Early bear, 13″, pale gold mohair, straw stuffed, fully jointed glass eyes, embroidered floss nose and claws (4 threads), growler, felt pads on long (2¾″) feet, small hump, long arms (7″) and snout. The overalls are most becoming. Note: nose treatment helps to make him unique. Some people feel that Steiff embroidered this "life-like" nose on their Teddies. This style is well known on Steiff stuffed animals. Courtesy Marlene Wendt. $350.00 up.

Three bears: Left, 10″, gold long pile mohair, all straw, fully jointed, shoe button eyes, upturned snout, black floss nose, mouth, claws, squeaker. Well made, probably American from 1920's. Courtesy Mary Grisby. $165.00 up. Center white, 12″, long pile white mohair, straw and sawdust stuffed, glass eyes, floss nose, mouth, claws, felt pads. He has had a new tie for every Christmas since 1926. Note arms and feet are getting shorter. Courtesy of original owner, Louise Schroer. $175.00. Irresistible bear, 10″, the rarity factors include: long pile snow white mohair, triangular head, long feet and arms. The short torso, long legs also set this early bear apart. Choice small size in original condition. Courtesy Mary Grisby. $350.00 up.

Smug Bear, 12″, gold mohair, all straw, black shoe button eyes close-set to give the cute expression, floss nose and downward mouth, and claws, upturned snout. Circa 1920. Celluloid Bull Dog circa 1915. $20.00-25.00. Courtesy Hazel Mathews. $185.00-200.00.

Steiff: 10″, thick pile soft gold mohair, straw stuffed, glass eyes, floss nose, mouth and claws, felt pads on big feet, long snout and arms. An unusually large hump distinguishes this sweet bear who for years was used as a puppet in a first grade classroom. The loving that he has gotten from hundreds of little ones has not altered his beautiful coat. Circa 1910. Courtesy Roberta Viscusi. $400.00.

A delightful bear with astonishing bright eyes: 16", light gold mohair, cork stuffed (heavier bear), fully jointed, glass eyes, black twill nose, floss mouth and claws, triangular head, long snout, acute hump, pink felt pads, no squeaker. A fine example of American origin. Childhood bear of Blanche Grieb born in 1896. Courtesy of her daughter, Naomi Stanton. $450.00 up.

Long pile burnished gold mohair; 15", all straw, black wooden shoe button eyes, felt pads, long feet, long snout, ears are sewn on laterally (English type), fully jointed. The floss nose could be reworked. Different pre 1920 Teddy. Courtesy Betty Shelley. $250.00-300.00 up.

Unusual bear: 21″, pale gold long pile mohair, straw and kapok stuffed, original felt pads on very long and slender feet, nose and mouth missing, no claws, markedly long arms with curved paws, acute hump. Early celluloid buttons replaced the eyes long ago. Circa 1910; but fits into no known identification table. Probably made by any of the 12 American companies that manufactured bears before 1912. (Author). $550.00-600.00.

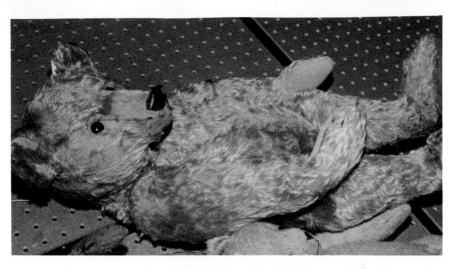

1915 Steiff, 24", pewter ear button/ff underscored, long pile honey mohair, all straw, shoe button eyes, black floss nose, mouth and claws, felt pads, long feet and arms, acute hump, fully jointed. Given new to John D. Ferry in 1915. Since then "Alice" has raised four children: the original owner, his two sisters and his daughter, the present owner. Courtesy Phyllis F. Gilbertson. $500.00 up.

A deserved favorite of every collector: 1915 Steiff, 24", feet 5½", honey long pile mohiar, all straw, hard leather shoe button eyes, black embroidered nose, mouth and claws, felt pads, fully jointed. With normal settling of the straw the body is so flexible that the bear can assume any attitude. Although somewhat worn this bear has a "Take me home" look. Courtesy Diane Hoffman. $500.00 up, this condition in large size.

Playmates: Left, 12″ gold short pile mohair, straw/kapok stuffed, shoe button eyes, early triangular head, light orange floss nose and claws, replaced brown cotton pads, fully jointed. Tends to be gimpy as both feet point in same direction. A less expensive bear circa 1915. Now $175.00-200.00. Right, 17″ gold mohair/pink cast, all kapok stuffing, fully jointed with hardwood discs, shoe button eyes, black floss nose, no claws. Long feet with triangular felt pads, low set long arms, long snout, modified hump. Finest quality. Circa 1910. (Author). $350.00 up.

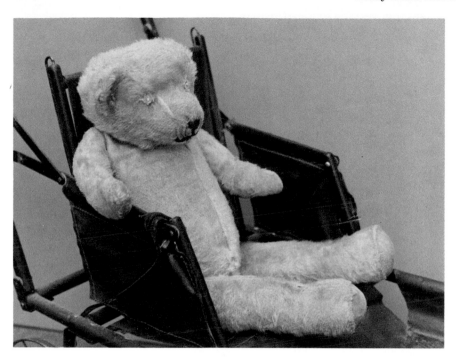

Rare Electric Eye bear: 21″, light
gold mohair, straw filled, rigid
neck to encase wires running to
battery pack in rear torso, jointed
arms that are shorter than those
of the era, jointed legs, stubby feet
with original leather pads. The
original batteries were found wrapped in heavy black paper forming
a pack ¾″ thick, 2″ wide and 2½″
tall, still in good condition. Quite
easily a new battery pack with tog-
gle switch and new light bulbs
replaced the original to working
condition. The seam in back must
be opened to change batteries.
Childhood bear of Violet Goold
born in 1907. When she received
this for Christmas the family
discovered the cat was terrified of
the eyes. Her older brother
delighted in chasing the cat,
flashing the bears eyes at it.
Courtesy Violet Goold. $350.00.

Another version of the rare electric eye bear; jointed head and arms, rigid legs, battery pack in back of head with switch in left ear. 22″, gold mohair, replaced pads, one eye (original bulb in socket), brown yarn nose and mouth, lead ring in nose. Courtesy Rosella and Tony Santopietro. With a little restoration, $350.00 up.

The extreme rarity of this electric eye novelty bear is rivalled by its visual appeal. 23″, inset red, white and blue mohair, all straw, hard stuffed, no claws, heavy black thread embroidered nose and mouth. White flannel pads, tiny replaced lightbulbs, short jointed arms, original imitation leather collar. Electric eye animals were patented in 1907 and continued in limited numbers until 1918. Ranging from bears, dogs, cats and monkeys to strange rabbits, they were never satisfactory as toys, but found their way into homes as parlor decorations. Battery activated by shaking the right paw or pressure on back. This bear would be hard to replace at any price. Courtesy Marlene Wendt. $450.00 up.

Patriotic red, white and blue bear; probably made by the Art Novelty Co. in 1908. 18″, (also made in other sizes), all straw, original glass stick pin eyes, felt pads, jointed arms only. Both unplayed with and unique. Courtesy Hazel Mathews. $400.00 up.

One in a thousand: rare black bear, circus type; 26″ head cir., 20″ tall, black mohair, all straw, disc jointed at head and arms, rigid legs, glass eyes, tan canvas pads, no claws, twill nose, embroidered mouth, no voice box. Long feet (5½″), white leather original collar with antique rivet closure. Original owner born in 1915. Every bear collector would like an old black Teddy Bear in their collection. However, the rarity factor is 1 in a 1000, computed on a sampling of 1000 old bears. He has great presence. Courtesy Margaret Klawuhn. $500.00 up.

German import, possibly Gebruder Sussenguth Novelty Co; 13″, unusual mohair blend of brown and beiges (also made in greys), all straw stuffed, fully jointed with cardboard discs. Brown glass eyes almost hidden in the fur, flesh color felt pads, black floss nose, mouth, claws with three long stitches each paw. Extremely long arms and feet, hump and squeaker. Note laid back ears and doll shape of body which dresses nicely. Of great interest to collectors; adds variety with color. Circa 1915. Courtesy Evelyn Krause. $450.00 up.

24″ light gold mohair, fully jointed, all straw, beige felt pads, long feet, curved arms, glass eyes, twill nose, floss mouth, big ears sewn low on head, no claws. Ideal type. $450.00 up. *The Browns, A Book of Bears,* verses by B. Parker, illustrated by N. Parker, W. & R. Chambers, Ltd. Great Britain, 1907. A delightful, rare, early book. All courtesy Marian Swartz. $185.00.

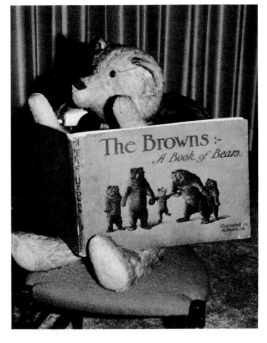

Super Teddy, 25", white mohair, firmly stuffed with straw (making heavy in this size), fully jointed, glass eyes, black twill nose, floss mouth, oversize floppy ears, flannel pads, long snout. This species of Teddy is usually found in very large sizes. Dressed in popular sailor motif with antique T.R. pin. Reading *The Teddy Bears,* by Adah Louise Sutton, copt. 1907, delightful adventures of a girl with her family of bears. Courtesy Marlene Wendt. Bear $450.00-500.00. Rare book $95.00.

Fillmore is a good listener, note the large ears on this 23" gold mohair, all straw, fully jointed, dark glass eyes, twill nose/floss mouth, no claws, growler, American circa 1918. Courtesy Roberta Viscusi. $400.00.

Charming: 12″ sagged to 11″, honey color mohair, head straw stuffed, body and limbs stuffed with sawdust making for a heavy bear, brown glass eyes, long snout and hump. Floss nose, mouth and claws, fully jointed. Clothes are original to bear; made from circa 1910 men's cotton stockings, using one sock for suit, stitched at crotch, one for muffler and one for stocking cap. Courtesy Nancy Roeder. $350.00.

13″ white long pile mohair, deep set shoe button eyes, brown velvet nose (unusual), brown floss mouth and claws, velvet pads, squeaker, long arms and hump with small head, long snout. Shows the early introduction of velvet for pads. Finest quality circa 1915. $350.00 up. Right: a pleasing greenish cast to the gold mohair, 11″, all straw, glass eyes, upturned long *aristocratic* snout, long arms, black floss over brown twill nose (unusual), floss mouth, no claws, felt pads/cardboard innersoles. Circa 1910. (Author). $350.00 up in this mint condition.

Rare large size of this most desirable bear: 24" beige long pile silky mohair, straw stuffed, fully jointed, shoe button eyes, black embroidered nose, mouth and claws, long snout, no squeaker, long feet and arms, hump. Gift to an uncle in 1911. Courtesy Lee Bryant. $500.00 up.

Variation on the "Three Bears" theme: Mama, 22" light gold mohair, all straw, black embroidered nose and wide mouth, claws, long snout and feet, shorter arms. Original bell at neck. Purchased recently in Paris, France. Circa before 1920. $275.00 up. Papa, 23", Steiff with ear button, grey-gold mohair, all straw, large shoe button eyes, brown floss nose, mouth and claws, hump, long snout, felt pads on long feet. A fine example of a 1915 Steiff in mint condition. $500.00-600.00. Baby, 13", gold mohair, all straw, fully jointed, replaced shoe button eyes, black embroidered nose in a horizontal line, short arms, no claws, round felt pads - all serving as distinguishing characteristics. Courtesy Virginia Lillard. $115.00.

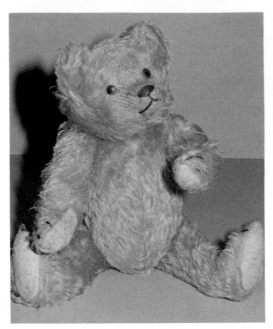

14″ long pile gold mohair, all straw, glass eyes, floss nose, mouth and claws, felt pads, long feet and curved arms, fully jointed. Snout is *very* long with a nice taper. There is a strong possibility that this Teddy was manufactured with the shaved snout. Circa 1912-15. Courtesy Teddy Fonseca. $275.00-300.00 up.

Steiff, 14″, lt. gold mohair, all straw, fully jointed, amber glass eyes, floss nose and mouth, no claws, felt pads. Note his exaggerated snout. The charming bear can fit any situation. Courtesy Kay Bransky. $450.00 up.

Childhood toy; almost a miniature, 9″, beige long pile mohair, all straw, rigid neck, jointed limbs, clear glass (one) eye/black pupil, tan floss nose, no claws or pads, sewn on ears, long snout. This well made and compact bear has a unique personality. Teddy still makes its den with original owner born in 1905. Shows how early in the century small bears were made with rigid necks. Courtesy Dorothy Altfather. $150.00 up.

Poker Face: 21″ gold mohair, all straw, fully jointed, glass eyes, oversized ears giving character; nose and mouth have been reworked, and felt pads replaced with canvas. Dressed with great imagination and attention to detail by Betty A. Kremp. American. Circa 1915. Courtesy Rosella and Tony Santopietro. $400.00 in set-up.

Mrs. Theodore Roosevelt: 23″ long pile gold mohair, all straw, glass eyes, long snout, black floss nose, mouth and claws, replaced canvas pads, well rounded hips. There must always be the *right* clothes for the *right* bear. This has been done most appropriately by Betty A. Kremp, using antique silk cape trimmed in silk lace, boa is a black plume, antique hat pin and broach, original T.R. button, antique flag ribbon. Choice because of the size and costuming. Courtesy Rosella and Tony Santopietro. $450.00.

Very special bear: has his family "wrapped around his paw." 20" Steiff (prong marks and circle imprint from button are apparent), mohair only on tips of ears, stuffed with cork, sawdust and straw, fully jointed, brown glass eyes, felt pads, black claw threads, black thread nose. Some consider excess love adds charm. It is more aesthetic with *no* fur than splotchy remains thereof. A symbol of survival. Without wear his value would be double. Courtesy Wanda Loukides. $250.00.

Sailor cloth type: 23", glass eyes, all straw, fully jointed, black twill nose, floss mouth, no claws, felt pads. Appears to be commercially made (and not from a pattern) in pre 1920 style with large triangular head and curved arms. There is no evidence inside of seams that bear ever had fur. Courtesy Mary Grisby. $200.00 up.

Ring Toss: Left, 17"/43 cm. pale gold mohair, all straw, original shoe button eyes, black floss nose and 5 claws (a bear has 4 claws *in vivo*) smallish head, long snout partially collapsed, replaced brown cotton pads, longish thick feet, hump, fully jointed. Circa 1915. $350.00.

23" early American, thick short pile gold mohair, all straw, glass eyes, black embroidered floss nose and mouth, exaggerated long snout and hump, head curved in back, curved arms, longish feet, no claws fully jointed. (Author). $350.00-400.00.

Bear on sled: 10", white mohair, all straw, black shoe button eyes, black embroidered nose, triangular head, suede pads. Stocking cap, mittens and scarf knit for this bear. Patsy Ann red rubber boots. The addition of high boots on a bear is appealing and sometimes hides flaws. Courtesy Shirlee Glass. $175.00 in this scene.

Curly supersoft long mohair (true angora mohair that appears not to have been spun), 18″, all straw with kapok and straw soft torso, large brown glass eyes, long snout, black floss nose, mouth and claws, triangular felt pads, squeaker, fully jointed. Angora has always been costly. This long pile would make the bear expensive even in 1915-20. This is an outstanding example, enough to make anyone addictive to Teddy Bear collecting. Courtesy Diane Hoffman. $400.00 up.

Shy Bear, 12″, lt. golden mohair, all straw, black shoe button eyes, floss nose/mouth and claws, felt pads. Feet are getting shorter in the 1912-20 period. $350.00. 7″ horse, wool over paper mache (1890-1904), carved wooden hooves, platform on cast iron spoked wheels. Courtesy Hazel Mathews. $125.00.

Doll's bear, 13″, beige mohair, straw stuffed, fully jointed, black shoe button eyes, floss nose, mouth and feet, felt pads, growler, long arms and snout, feet are becoming shorter 1915-20. Courtesy Susan Passarelli. $300.00.

Early American Teddy: 15″ lt. gold mohair, straw/kapok stuffed, small triangular head, floss nose/mouth and claws, long feet/felt oval pads, squeaker, acute hump, shoulders set low. Circa 1915. Yes/No Elephant, 8″ high, grey felt, shoe button eyes, rayon covered straw tusks, original circus blanket, marked "Schuco" on bronze painted metal wheels. 1920's. $250.00 up. Often proper display with another toy can showcase a bear's special charm. (Author). Bear, $250.00 up.

Snow white thick pile mohair aptly named "Snowball," 16½″, straw head, cotton body, fully jointed, glass eyes, leatherized cloth pads suggesting European origin, circa 1920. Very desirable antique bear was birthday gift from husband. Courtesy Tammie Depew. $300.00-350.00.

Enigmatic celluloid disc eyes rimmed in metal: 18″, gold mohair, all straw, black twill nose, embroidered mouth, no claws, long snout, original felt pads, fully jointed. A rarely found bear; probably origin Gebruder Sussenauth, Germany, circa 1925. Wearing child's celluloid belt with rattle, dated: "Pat. 1920," decorated with five playtime pictures. Courtesy Rosella and Tony Santopietro. $450.00-500.00.

Teacher: 22", off white mohair, all straw, glass eyes, long *upturned* snout, long arms with curved paws, felt pads. Circa 1920. Eyeglasses are a pleasing accessory to Teddys and cost a great deal less than the bear! Reading "The Traveling Bears" by Seymour Eaton from that series of 10 published by Barse & Hopkins, 1909-21. $75.00. (Author). Bear, $300.00-350.00.

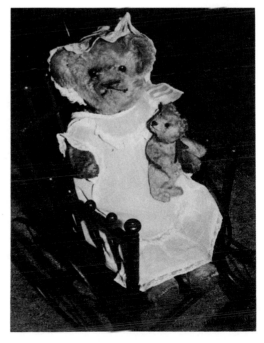

Beige mohair, 21", all straw, glass eyes, round burlap pads, short arms, pointed snout, fully jointed. Probably American made. A fine bear, circa 1915-20, appealing in this size. $275.00. 6" beige mohair, straw stuffed, brown floss nose, glass eyes, long feet, fully jointed. German. Courtesy Marian Swartz. $135.00 up.

White long pile mohair, 18″, straw and kapok stuffed, brown glass eyes, long snout, pink embroidered nose and claws, pink felt pads, fully jointed, squeaker. Since white bears were manufactured in a ratio of 1:25 to gold, this bear can be termed rare. Circa 1910-20. Courtesy Diane Hoffman. $450.00 up.

Left: Wide face bear, 14½″, pale gold mohair, hard stuffed straw, fully jointed, shoe button eyes, wide black floss nose, mouth and claws, medium size hump, pointy felt pads, wide gusset at end gives distinctive look. $250.00 up.

Pale gold mohair, 15½″, straw stuffed, fully jointed, black shoe button eyes, black floss nose, mouth and claws, tan felt pads. Note shaved (not worn) snout, fatter body with huge hump, large ears stick out to give an innocent look. Courtesy Marlene Wendt. $350.00.

26″ gold mohair, all straw stuffed, shoe button eyes, black floss nose, mouth and claws, original felt pads, long feet and long curved arms. Perfectly shaped Teddy Bear with skillful modelling. Given to original owner when she was 1 year old in 1922. The toy was too large for her at that time and subsequently has never been played with. This beloved bear is proudly displayed in his own high chair in the dining room of owner Cecilia Burkhardt. No button evident but suggests Steiff. This giant treasure in new condition, $700.00 up.

Excellent American quality: 22″, long pile gold mohair, firmly stuffed with straw, glass eyes (replaced), black embroidered nose, mouth and claws, long snout, longish feet and long curved arms (replaced pads), fully jointed. Dating 1920 exactly. From original owner, Herbert Freiberg. $195.00 up.

Rare Mechanical Bears: 19″, made in Germany in early 1920's for J.R. Larson Dept. Stores display titled, "Animals Enjoy Christmas Too." The bear playing the piano and the dancing bear are two from thirty five pieces. Motors are ingenious and simple. Composition covered with early plush, glass eyes. One of a kind. Courtesy Berdie C. Hupper. $500.00 each.

Dr. O'Bear, 14″ gold mohair, all straw, fully jointed, original glass eyes (close set), black floss embroidered nose, replaced pads, no voice box. Note: large bat-like ears sewn on. Purchased new in 1920 for Dr. Philip Gordy, former Professor of Neurosurgery at Jefferson Hospital in Philadelphia. Original owner gave bear to his daughter who appropriately dressed him in scrub clothes. Courtesy Nanci Burney. $350.00 up.

"I am Loved," 15", gold mohair, all straw, fully jointed, shoe button eyes, floss nose and smiling mouth, no claws, replaced felt pads, long feet and arms, upturned pointed snout. Personality plus! Childhood bear of owner born in 1923. Courtesy Jim Murray. $200.00-250.00.

9½" Steiff with credentials: early gold mohair, all straw, fully jointed, black shoe button eyes, floss nose/mouth and claws, beige felt pads, long curved arms, big feet, skinny ankles (as found in 1920's bears), hump on back. Went to Stanford University and must like football. He has scores of games between Cal and Stanford and the year written on all 4 pads. Years are 1923 through 1926. These notations on pads add interest and value. Courtesy Wanda Loukides. $400.00 up.

Clown Bear: 9", woolly plush, shades of browns and white to give natural appearance, all straw, glass eyes, beige felt pads, long feet, brown embroidered nose and mouth, original clown hat (stuffed) sewn on, fully jointed, A well made and *rare* (novelty) bear in desirable small size. Probable maker: Gebruder Sussenguth, Germany. Circa 1920-30. Mint condition. Courtesy Marian Swartz. $250.00 up.

Blank look Teddy Bear: 13", short pile mohair, all straw, clear glass eyes with dark pupil, twill nose, mouth missing, no claws. Note his unusual ears. $200.00. Swivel neck dog, 7", "Teddy Bear" gold mohair, all straw, glass eyes. Circa 1930. Courtesy Hazel Mathews. $65.00 up.

Bought from a peddler in December 1924. Bellhop Bear, 16″, mohair head and feet, hard stuffed cotton, fully jointed, shoe button eyes, long snout, embroidered nose and claws, brown felt hands and foot pads, long feet sewn on red/black felt uniform. Played with by three generations and still communicates Yes/No. Attests to the quality of the early products. The Schuco Bellhop monkey is more common than the bear. Courtesy Ruby Hinegardner. In worn condition, $250.00.

Endearing Schuco "Yes/No" bear; 11″ rare small size, long pile light gold mohair, all straw, fully jointed, glass eyes, black floss nose and mouth, felt pads. The chances of finding an original tag on any bear are slim, much less a circa 1925-35 mechanical. This one is encased in plastic and printed in English, French, Italian and Spanish. NPA.

103

Smart "Yes/No" bear with cute upturned snout, 13″, light gold mohair, straw stuffed, fully jointed, black shoe button eyes which indicate this is one of the earliest versions of these various German "Schuco" mechanicals. Distinctive floss nose and mouth, long curved arms, fatter torso and slender arms, squeaker. Every collector wants at least one communicative bear and are willing to pay more than the rarity factor indicates. Handmade overalls original to bear. Courtesy Marlene Wendt. $350.00.

The Schuco Co. was founded in Nurnberg, Germany in 1912. The first toys had *clockwork* mechanisms activated by *winding* a tail or leg. This later example used tail as lever to move head in any direction: 12″, blonde mohair, all straw, brown glass eyes, black floss nose and claws, pink felt pads, fully jointed. Still functions today as most of these well made German mechanicals do. Circa late 1920's-on. Courtesy Beverly L. Krein. $275.00 up.

Anatomy of a Teddy Bear, 13″, no fur, all straw, glass eyes, floss nose and mouth, pointed snout, no claws, squeaker. Years of pressing squeaker created forward curvature of the spine. Circa 1920. Courtesy Suelynn Gustafson. $100.00.

Friends: Left, 16″, light gold long curly mohair, straw head, soft torso and limbs, glass eyes, long snout (worn) shows wear first, reworked stitched nose and mouth, no claws, felt pads, long arms, squeaker. American circa 1920-30. (Author). $300.00. 14″, very long angora mohair, long snout, straw head, soft torso and limbs, floss nose and mouth, no claws, glass eyes, pointy velvet pads. Circa 1920-30. (Author). $250.00.

White thick bristle mohair, 24", all straw hard stuffed, original small glass eyes, long snout, black floss nose, mouth and claws, pink felt pads on stubby feet, probably American. Mint condition in rare white color. Circa 1915-20. Courtesy Diane Hoffman. $300.00 up.

20" deep gold mohair, all straw stuffing. original shoe button eyes, original felt pads, long snout. Excellent quality American bears in mint condition are becoming very hard to find. $300.00. Sitting dog: 7½" possible early Steiff Collie, well contoured curved haunches, a hallmark of Steiff, all straw stuffed, blk. embroidered nose and long feet. $75.00. Small bear: 7", fully jointed, cotton plush, glass bead eyes, Poland 1970's. $10.00. All courtesy Marian Swartz.

106

Old "Mr. Wheatly," 26″, gold mohair, all straw, fully jointed, glass eyes, floss nose and mouth, felt pads. Imaginative photograph. Photographing Teddy Bears can be a hobby in itself. Circa 1920's Courtesy Kay Bransky. $300.00.

Charming "Old Fellow;" note the wonderful amber color of the old glass eyes. The replacement eyes sold today cannot match the antique ones. 15", soft gold mohair, all straw, fully jointed. Circa 1920. Courtesy Roberta Viscusi. $200.00-250.00.

Bear on Bearskin, 13", long pile shaggy gold mohair, straw stuffed, fully jointed, shoe button eyes, cream felt pads, floss nose and mouth, hump, upturned snout gives a mouse-like appearance emphasized by small ears. Bearskin, silk ruffled trim on 2 long sides, $15.00; Block has glass and metal bell, $5.00. Courtesy Nan C. Moorehead. Bear. $200.00.

Commercially made bear: 12″ brown worsted/nap, all straw, fully jointed, one replaced faceted button eye, one original shoe button eye, brown floss nose, mouth and claws, felt pads squeaker. $200.00 up. Playful and composed with 6″ 1890 papier mache rocking horse. Courtesy Hazel Mathews. $65.00.

Nuances of comedy in this 14″ all straw stuffed donkey, earliest gold rayon plush stationary head, glass stick pin eyes, pink flannel lined long ears, muslin torso, velvet limbs with sewn joints. Dressed in orig. orange and green cotton flannel pinned-on overalls and jacket. Very rare. Circa 1910. $125.00 up. "See-Saw", sand toy, 7″ high, circa 1930s, marked *Chein, U.S.A.*, $35.00.
Large gold short pile mohair, 24″, all straw, glass eyes, floss nose (horizontal), mouth and claws, long thick feet, modified hump, short arms, long snout. American. Circa 1915-25. (Author). $300.00.

A different bear: 13″, brown fabric/nap (this fabric was often used for Teddy Bears circa 1920), straw stuffed, fully jointed, shoe button eyes, peach color felt pads, brown thread nose, hump, pointy feet and curved up paws. Knitted sweater added. Courtesy Wanda Loukides. $300.00.

23″ gold mohair, all straw stuffed with straw settling out of snout, black embroidered nose, facial tears sewn with black thread giving the appearance of scars. Full of personality. Football-type bag torso, hump, curved arms, stubby feet, fully jointed. One wishes that this Teddy could tell of his adventures. Circa 1920. Courtesy Marian Swartz. $200.00 up.

Circa 1925: Velvet circus bear-type, 30", unjointed, gold cotton plush head, soft stuffed torso and arms, straw stuffed legs, self fabric pads/cardboard innersoles, yellow flannel-felt hands, sewn on suit, gold trim. Glass eyes, nose is brown cotton pom pom, rayon cord embroidered mouth. Missing gold hat. Note especially long snout on this impressive bear. Courtesy Diane Hoffman. $225.00 up.

Rarely found character circus bear has historical significance in bear chronology, 22" early yellow plush and sewn on flannel-felt clothes. Celluloid disc eyes that became available in 1925, prong type attachment. Red metal prong-type nose, embroidered smiling mouth line stitch. Suit is decorated with same metal buttons painted yellow. Circa 1925. (Author). $75.00 up.

Gold bristle mohair: 18", all straw hard stuffed, small glass eyes, embroidered nose and claws, felt pads on longish feet. Well made with ears sewn on. Popular bear in the stores at the time circa 1920-30. American. Courtesy Diane Hoffman. $195.00 in mint condition and this larger size.

Well traveled bear pair: Left, 16", white mohair straw stuffed, fully jointed, glass eyes, long snout, embroidered nose and mouth, claws at one time, tan felt pad (one), others replaced to match, squeaker; note small ears. Dressed in antique flannel and lace. $175.00. 16", 1920's gold mohair, straw stuffed, fully jointed, shoe button eyes, replaced felt pads, round feet, floss nose and mouth, no claws. Note: triangular shaped ears, pointed snout and skinny arms and legs. $150.00. Paper covered wooden humpback trunk, $40.00. Today there is a revival of the rage for clothing Teddy. All courtesy Nan C. Morehead.

Mama Bear: 12″, gold mohair, all straw, eyes replaced by embroidery, embroidered silk floss nose, mouth and claws. Thin legs, oval felt pads, circa 1925. $150.00 up.

Baby: 8″ mohair head straw stuffed, canvas torso and limbs pin jointed, straw and cotton stuffed, no pads, glass eyes, embroidered nose and mouth. Unusual small bear. Courtesy Betty Shelley. $75.00.

Oversize ears set low suggest one of the first examples made by Alpha Farnell, England. 16″ thick pile golden mohair, straw stuffed, full jointed, black shoe button eyes, black floss nose, mouth and claws, felt pads, acute hump, long snout. Wonderfully expressive bear. Pigeon-toed when standing. English circa 1910. Has a "character" look. $350.00 up. Unexpected color: "Holly" so named because of Christmas red mohair, 17″ firmly straw stuffed, fully jointed, glass eyes, floss nose, mouth and claws, squeaker, slender arms and legs, slight hump, white felt pads recovered with muslin. This 1915-25 American bear is made choice and desirable by its bright red covering. Nice bear to find in your Christmas stocking. Scarce. Courtesy Marlene Wendt. $325.00 up.

Left: owner's childhood bear, "Ted," 15" brown mohair, soft stuffed, fully jointed, squeaker, floss nose and mouth, no claws. The mother removed the glass eyes when child was small (as many mothers did). They were replaced recently. The Teddy cost 98 cents during the Depression, 1935 to be exact. Now, $135.00. Hard to find red/white and blue bear, 15", all mohair, straw stuffed, *fully jointed*, clear glass eyes/black pupil, brown floss nose and mouth, front paws white mohair, foot pads blue mohair. Brass studs on chest. Attractive bear to a child or collector. He can be whatever you imagine, bell hop, cadet or circus bear. Imaginative use of color circa 1920. All courtesy Marlene Wendt. $300.00 up.

Rich gold brushed mohair, resembling mohair upholstery fabric, 24", fully jointed, well stuffed with straw, shoe button eyes, long snout, floss nose/mouth, replaced pads, large sewn on ears, probable American origin circa 1920's. This large Teddy can be dressed effectively. Courtesy Marian Swartz. $275.00.

Lime green Teddy; 19" (large size for this type), mohair, straw head and limbs, soft torso with squeeze music box. In the most expensive models growlers were replaced by Swiss music boxes resting in a bed of cotton. Brown glass eyes, black stitched nose, mouth and claws, flesh color felt pads, long feet and curved long arms, small hump. Excellent body contouring. The music box was the rage of 1920-30. *Crank type* music box in bears back is oldest (1907) style. Courtesy Beverly L. Krein. $300.00.

Chartreuse 18" mohair, all straw, floss nose and mouth, no claws, stubby arms, white flannel pads, purple crepe bow and eyes to match. Circa 1920. Toy ten pins, soldiers, 6½", 1920's, set of 10 with 2 bowling balls. Courtesy Hazel Mathews. Bear, $250.00.

Pink mohair bear, 12", all straw, fully jointed, glass eyes, floss nose, mouth, round felt pads, squeaker. Note unusually large head and short arms give him an off-balance look. American circa 1920-30. Courtesy Tammie Depew. $200.00 up.

Red sparse bristle mohair (what he misses in fur cover he makes up for in the elegant wool antique tuxedo), 13", all straw, glass eyes, ears sliced into head, no claws on this skinny bear, short arms, short feet, flannel pads, squeaker. Japan circa 1920-30. $95.00 dressed. *The Traveling Bears in Outdoor Sports* book, published by Barse & Hopkins, 1915, one of a series. Courtesy Lenora Schweitzberger. $65.00.

116

Long pile, rich natural brown mohair, 15″, all straw, fully jointed, glass eyes, black twill nose, floss mouth, no claws (in late twenties bears began to lose the claws due to the shorter feet). Excellent American quality in a life-like color. Courtesy Carolyn M. Altfather. $195.00.

English bear, circa 1920, 20″, gold mohair, all straw, glass eyes, floss nose, no claws, felt pads (note the bandage to surgeon's specifications), long snout/large head, original blue silk bow. Purchased in London in 1978. First edition of Seymour Eaton's *The Roosevelt Bears, Their Travel and Adventures* copt. Edward Stern & Co., Inc. 1906. (Author). Bear $275.00. Book $125.00.

Football-shape torso, 21", gold short pile thick mohair, all straw, fully jointed, replaced shoe button eyes, long snout, black embroidered nose, no claws, stubby feet, replaced canvas pads. American. Circa 1920's. Courtesy Marian Swartz. $250.00.

Little Jewel: 9", silver-grey long pile mohair, all straw, shoe button eyes, black floss nose, mouth and claws, long snout, felt pads, long feet, hump, fully jointed. Circa 1910. $275.00. Right: 19", caramel thick short pile mohair, all straw, twill nose, black embroidered mouth, shoe button eyes, longish feet, velvet pads, voice box, fully jointed. (Author). $275.00.

Gold short pile mohair 24″, all straw, fully jointed/cardboard discs, shoe button eyes, traces of floss nose and mouth, old wool scraps mend pads, hump, football shape tummy. This style of American 1920 bear is usually found in a large size. Courtesy Evelyn Krause. $275.00.

Two American Teddys. Red Coat, 21″, long pile gold mohair, all straw, fully jointed, glass eyes, embroidered floss nose (horizontal) and mouth, no claws, long snout. Well made 1920. $350.00.

Automobile goggles made of metal and leather: 22″ short pile gold mohair, all straw, fully jointed, long snout, elongated torso, original shoe button eyes, floss nose and mouth. Old cotton stocking material sewn on as pads. Circa 1920. (Author). $300.00.

Seated: Fine quality, gold bristle mohair 20″, all straw, cut in ears, glass eyes with glass stem, floss nose, mouth, claws, large snout, large shoulders, pink felt pads, stubby feet. Reserved British look. $300.00. Standing: 18″ soft grey mohair, all straw, floss nose/mouth, no claws, no squeaker, replaced suede pads. Courtesy Hazel Mathews. $275.00.

17″ bear of highest quality: snow white thick pile mohair, all straw, fully jointed, original glass eyes, pink embroidered nose and mouth, canvas pads, voice box, no claws, wonderful ears. More rounded heads emerging in late 1920's-30. A lucky find in this pristine condition. Courtesy Rosella and Tony Santopietro. $275.00-300.00.

Telephone Teddies: red sweater (commonly found on Teddy Bears) 16″ caramel bristle mohair, firmly stuffed with straw, black twill nose, upturned snout, blk. floss mouth, ears sewn on, felt pads/stubby feet. Eyes replaced with white shoe buttons instead of black, fully jointed. This less expensive Teddy of the 1920's is possibly the type given as a premium for 1-4 subscriptions to *Youth's Companion, Needlecraft Magazine* and others. $200.00. 17″, thick caramel short pile mohair, all straw, brown glass eyes, brown twill nose, black embroidered mouth, long snout, felt pads, no claws, American. These unusual Teddy Bear ears were seen in *The Youth's Companion*, 1923. (Author). $200.00.

Thin bear, 15″, gold short pile mohair, all straw, sliced in ears, (occasionally the English firms took this short cut), glass eyes, black embroidered nose, claws, longer snout and appealing look. Excellent quality. $175.00. Friend is 12″ all mohair rabbit with inset markings, glass eyes, pink nose, no claws or pads, fully jointed. Courtesy Rosella and Tony Santopietro. NPA.

Steam roller bear: 18″, ginger colored short thick pile mohair (a darker, more unusual, early color), hard stuffed straw, fully jointed, shoe button eyes, longish snout, black floss nose/mouth, short arms, replaced pads, stubby feet. Probably American origin. Steam roller circa 1920's. $125.00. Courtesy Nancy Nelson. Bear $185.00 up.

White-turned-grey bristle mohair, 10″, straw stuffed, fully jointed, replaced plastic eyes that are too large, felt pads, embroidered nose, mouth and claws, longish snout, squeaker, elongated torso, long 5½″ arms, curved paws, thin 4½″ legs, longish feet. Courtesy Linda Holsworth. $100.00.

Standing: 13" gold mohair, all straw stuffed, fully jointed, shoe button eyes, brown floss nose, sewn on ears, short arms (appears that left arm was cut off midway and transplanted to right side), squeaker. Unusual appearance. $95.00.

Seated: 12" gold mohair, all straw stuffed, fully jointed, black embroidered nose, round velvet pads, squeaker. Circa late 1920's. Courtesy Marian Swartz. $95.00.

Tuxedo, 15", sparse gold mohair, all straw, fully jointed, triangular head in old style, but of cheaper Japanese quality with ears sliced into head, glass eyes, black embroidered nose and claws, felt pads. Circa 1920-30. Wearing "Snoopy" clothes, popular now for old bears. Courtesy Nancy Hupper. $100.00.

Magician with the Paul Fox Cups and Balls. 21″ gold velour plush, hard stuffed straw, glass eyes, floss mouth/nose, no claws, felt pads. In new condition from 1920-30. (Author). $250.00.

19″, sparse gold mohair, pink fabric backing, all straw, glass eyes, longish snout, black floss nose, no mouth, black floss claws, pink velvet pads. Note the well shaped ankles and football torso reminiscent of Winnie the Pooh, 1920. Courtesy Carolyn Mathews. $175.00.

19″ cinnamon long pile mohair, straw head, soft torso and limbs, original glass eyes, floss nose, no claws, voice box. 1930's. Courtesy Hazel Mathews. $250.00.

Attractive 16" shaggy gold mohair, all straw, fully jointed, original glass eyes, black embroidered nose, mouth, claws, replaced felt pads (addition of shoes gives image of longer feet). Brings on smiles. Courtesy Marian Swartz. $150.00.

English twins: 14", late 1920's, gold mohair, straw head, kapok torso and limbs (kapok is favored by the English), fully jointed, large original amber glass eyes, imitation leather-type pads (another English characteristic), large black thread nose/mouth, squeaker, wide heads, pointy feet. Wearing cotton knit sunsuits, probably original to bears or added when first purchased. Add value for twinning. Courtesy Wanda Loukides. $450.00 for pair.

125

Two old veterans from 1920's. Left, 12″, gold mohair, all straw stuffed, shoe buttons replace the original glass eyes, missing nose and mouth, wobbly arm and weak leg. Childhood bear of Gilbert Tiger, born 1916. $75.00 this condition. Even worse off is 13″ gold mohair, all straw, round pads, head and neck are weak; original owner (pictured) died in 1923. The Teddy was then played with by Dorothy Mulholland (niece) until she was 14. $125.00 up if excellent condition. Now, $55.00. Key wind Drum Major, 14″, made by Wolverine, U.S.A. Courtesy Virginia Joy. $45.00 up.

Twins: 9″, light gold mohair, all straw. Bear on right has replaced eyes. Other has original clear glass/black pupil. Black embroidered nose, mouth and claws, no pads, fully jointed. Note that the claws are stitched on *outside* of center seam. Courtesy Diane Hoffman. As a matched pair possibly belonging to twins or siblings, $250.00-300.00.

Seated bear: 23″, gold mohair, thick short pile, all straw, fully jointed, glass eyes, replaced pads. He is the protector of all, gives advice to the younger and has his own place in the living room. Circa late 1920's. $250.00 up.

Standing: 21″ bright gold mohair, straw head, soft torso and limbs, fully jointed, glass eyes, shaved snout, floss nose and mouth , no claws, felt pads. American, 1930's. This size bear in mint condition is getting harder to find. $150.00 up.

Younger: 12″ gold mohair, all soft stuffed, fully jointed, glass eyes, no pads, excellent quality but a later bear, $75.00. All courtesy Marian Swartz.

Steiff with ear button, 15″, honey mohair, straw stuffed, fully jointed, long snout, pudgy tummy (developing in 1920-40 period), glass eyes, coarse brown thread nose, mouth and claws, beige felt pads, growler. The stern expression of this pristine bear adds variety to a collection. Courtesy Wanda Loukides. $350.00 up.

127

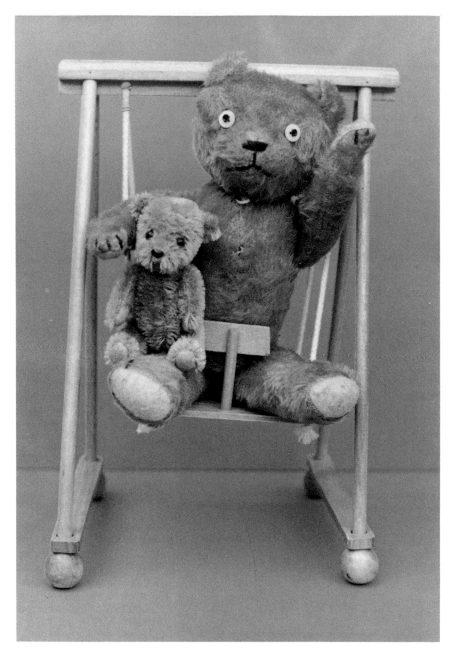

Modern, (predating contemporary), baby faced bear, 5½″, fully jointed, hard stuffed straw, beige mohair, flesh color felt pads, no claws, stick pin eyes, plastic nose distinguished by red felt tongue. Good example of quality. $15.00 up.

1920-30 bear: 13″, gold/brown mohair, all straw, fully jointed, black yarn nose, mouth and claws, felt pads, squeaker, replaced eyes. Of good but not impressive quality. Courtesy Beth Everhart. $95.00-125.00.

"Old Timer" purchased at the famous Swap Meet near Burnaby, B.C. 19″ gold bristle mohair, straw stuffed, glass eyes, longish snout, embroidered nose, mouth, claws, replaced cotton pads, voice box. Circa 1920-on, when arms became shorter and feet became thicker as well as shorter. Courtesy Margaret M. Carlson. $150.00 with wear.

"My Teddy" is from Australia, a high-quality British import given to original owner in 1929. 18″, gold long pile mohair, at one time frosted brown (residual color at jointings only remain after many baths). Straw head, kapok torso/limbs. Replaced glass (taxidermist) eyes. Felt pads replaced with suede of same color, cardboard innersoles, longer sheared-mohair snout, black satin stitched embroidered nose, mouth and claws (double thread line stitch), growler. Very sweet bear. Courtesy Ena Vogel. $200.00 up.

White mohair, 20″, hard stuffed cotton head, kapok torso and limbs, fully jointed, felt pads, no claws, replaced old eyes, black embroidered nose with an unusually wide mouth. Circa 1920-30, American. $225.00.

Astounding cat, 14″, yellow mohair, green glass eyes, pink embroidered nose, black claws, no pads, jointed arms and head. Tail forms a tripod for support. Rare. Courtesy Rosella and Tony Santopietro. $150.00 up.

Green bear, 13″, long pile mohair, all straw, brown glass eyes, black embroidered nose and claws, replaced pads, fully jointed. Includes a well-functioning music box (just squeeze tummy to activate). Superior materials and workmanship. Price was $5.00 in 1930. Especially sweet face. Courtesy original owner, Peg Derry. $125.00 up.

"Rosie" is a 16", well-worn, much mended armful of feminine charm. Pink rayon plush, fully jointed, cotton stuffed, replaced white felt pads, restored mouth and nose. Her receeding chin and bright shoe button eyes give her an appearance of sweet acceptance and resignation. Circa 1930's. $150.00 up because of wear. Black iron Teddy Bear, 2½", is a parking station for bubble gum. All courtesy Margaret M. Carlson, NPA.

Left: 14" pink cotton plush, all soft stuffed, fully jointed, glass eyes, black embroidered nose and mouth, no claws, white cotton felt pads, squeaker, well shaped body and limbs. Wearing his original blue ribbon. These colorful bears from 1930's are an intriguing fact of bear history. Made for a girl child no doubt. Of highest quality. $225.00 up. Right: bear with stubby snout (pug nose suggests English origin), 15", pink mohair, firmly straw stuffed, fully jointed, glass eyes, black embroidered nose and wide mouth, no claws, off white felt pads, working squeaker, long thin legs. Everyone needs at least one pink bear. Courtesy Marlene Wendt. $275.00 up.

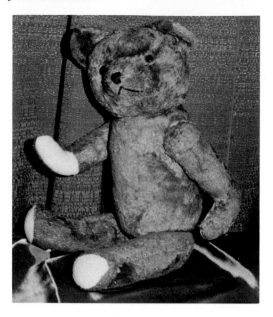

Before: 24″ cinnamon cotton plush, straw head, torso/limbs hard stuffed cotton, glass eyes, embroidered nose and mouth, snout turns upward, no claws, squeaker, unusual right angle position of upper paws. Undressed, $165.00. After: A bear of fashion; intriguing social documentary with a bear. Dressed in antique green silk beaded chiffon, crystal earbobs, braid headdress with feather plume, French beaded purse. The upward glancing eyes and "haute couture" of the 20's makes this bear most interesting. Courtesy Nan C. Moorehead. $250.00 up.

Worn and weary but still able to "smell the flowers". 17″, probably English, long pile gold mohair, brown velvet pads, head straw, torso/limbs soft, well patterned and fully jointed body has nicely curved and shaped arms, legs and head, with hump, floss nose/mouth, replaced glass eyes, growler. Courtesy Nan C. Moorehead. $190.00.

Large: 17″, gold long pile mohair with shaved inset snout, straw stuffed head, soft body, fully jointed, floss nose and mouth, felt pads, orange tin eyes with decals (in use a short time). $200.00 up. Owner's booties from 1927 on 12″ Teddy: gold mohair, fully jointed, glass eyes, remnants of floss nose and mouth, long curved arms and big feet. Circa 1920. Courtesy Bev Murray. $175.00.

Sports minded: Left, 13″ bright gold long pile mohair, straw/kapok, floss nose/mouth, no claws, felt pads, stubby feet, inset nose (shaved mohair). Scarce orange tin (decal) eyes. American, possibly Knickerbocker, 1930's. $185.00. Right, 15″, early cotton plush string-type, straw head, cotton torso/limbs, glass eyes, floss nose/mouth, no claws, squeaker. Stubby feet but a good athlete. 1930. (Author). $175.00.

Pince Nez bear, 16″, cotton plush and mohair, straw head, soft stuffed body, fully jointed, early plastic disc eyes, white felt pads, embroidered nose and mouth, nicely pointed dark brown mohair snout, hump, $125.00-150.00. Antique "Roosevelt Memorial Association" pin, $25.00; bear cart, $85.00. Tin eyed/decal bear, 19″, cotton plush, straw head, soft body, fully jointed, felt pads, embroidered nose and mouth. Note: oversize ears. Courtesy Nan C. Moorehead. $125.00-150.00. Older Golliwog, $85.00.

Exact dating from original owner, 1932. 12″ brown/cream mohair, straw stuffed, fully jointed, felt pads, shoe button eyes (shows extended use of shoe button eyes), inset long snout, embroidered nose, mouth and claws, short legs. An interesting example showing the evolution of the Teddy Bear. Courtesy Virginia Joy. $85.00 up.

"Helene", 18″, fully jointed, tawny short mohair, from Canada. Straw/cotton mix, black felt nose (heart-shaped), bright orange early plastic eyes, pads on upturned hands and feet of short pile brown mohair. Punched-in face suggests she may have been packed away for a long time. Working growler. Exaggerated ears give an interesting variation. Circa 1930's. Courtesy Margaret M. Carlson. $95.00 up.

Brown and yellow cotton plush, 10″, cotton stuffed, replaced eyes, embroidered floss nose and mouth, original *leather* pads (unusual), long snout, fully jointed. Circa 1930's. Has a comic appeal. Courtesy Sheri Carter. $65.00.

His deep-set shoe button eyes give him a look of concentration, possibly puzzlement. 14″ (large) orange rayon plush, straw stuffed, rigid neck, pin jointed limbs, embroidered nose/mouth, airbrushed claws, working squeaker, original rayon ribbon. Probable carnival bear made in Japan 1930-40. Some peopole like these. Courtesy Margaret M. Carlson. $75.00.

Enjoying a snack: 8″, plush, straw stuffed, fully jointed, embroidered nose, mouth and claws. Original collar and bell. Has a 1930's (Japanese) import "look." Courtesy Kay Bransky. $75.00.

Waif, a "nobody loves me" apologetic expression, 13″ panda, black and white mohair, cotton hard stuffed, fully jointed, original shoe button eyes indicate he was early circa 1915, black embroidered nose and mouth, no claws, black knitted pads. Note: eyes are not framed in black as is usual with a panda, and his black yoke on torso extends around back. Long snout not typical of the moon faced animal. Courtesy Margaret M. Carlson. $150.00 up.

English Panda: 14″, black/white long pile mohair, kapok stuffed, (popular stuffing in Great Britain). Black felt surrounds glass eyes backed in white felt, black stitched nose and mouth, long snout (unlike a Panda). Black felt pads, fully jointed and unusual. Courtesy Betty Shelley. $150.00.

Panda: 18″ white/black mohair, all straw, fully jointed, glass eyes with black felt backing, triangular head model, floss nose and mouth, tan pads. Pandas tend to soil easily. This one in excellent condition from late 1920's. Courtesy Beverly L. Krein. $150.00 up.

A *major* Teddy Bear: Steiff from 1930's. Steiff Teddy Bears have changed the least over the years; 14″ beige mohair, all straw, long snout, glass eyes, brown floss nose, mouth and claws, *beaver* felt pads, squeaker. Note more of the animal (bear) look, flattened at bridge of nose, elongated face. Hard to find this bear with identification. Chest tag, "Original Teddy." Courtesy Hazel Mathews. $400.00-450.00.

139

All hard cotton stuffed (cotton retains its shape better than straw), sturdy bear, 23″, rich cinnamon long pile mohair, glass eyes, floss nose and mouth, no claws, long thick feet, velvet pads and ear lining (used in 1930's) in contrasting color. He is a finer bear than his demand indicates. (Author). $135.00.

Whimsical: long pile white mohair, 15″, straw head, soft body, black floss nose and mouth, replaced silk button eyes, velvet pads. Shirley Temple era: $200.00-250.00. Cloth book, *Dollie's Sewing Bee*, copt. 1908 by the Saalfield Pub. Co. to make complete dolls and wardrobe (boy, girl and baby). Courtesy Hazel Mathews. $125.00.

Shirley Temple Type: circa 1938. Large cinnamon bear: 23″ finest quality long pile mohair, shaved longish snout, rounded head, replaced eyes, black floss nose, no claws. Original felt pads replaced with calico (missing pads reveal the typical 1930's grey/colors heavy cotton stuffing), straw stuffed head. With curved arms this fully jointed bear is more than equal the quality of earlier versions and will not show soil. Courtesy George L. Farinsky. $150.00.

Shirley Temple-type, 20″, long pile cinnamon mohair, shaved muzzle, glass eyes black floss nose and mouth, straw head and soft body, straw packed in torso at shoulder plate to hold large head erect, oval felt pads, no claws. Quizzical expression. Courtesy Hazel Mathews. $175.00.

Rich chocolate brown mohair, 38″, brown glass eyes, original beige velvet pads, all straw stuffed, fully jointed. The bear is massive. A wing nut instead of cotter pin was used on cardboard discs. Knickerbocker. Undoubtedly an expensive bear in the late 1930's. Courtesy Diane Hoffman. $350.00 up now.

Old English Teddy, 28″, named "Buster Bear," gold mohair, straw stuffed, fully jointed, glass eyes, floss nose and mouth, felt pads. Circa 1920-30. Obtained from estate sale in England. Riding 23″ high old straw stuffed glass eyed horse attributed to Steiff. Courtesy Kay Bransky. Bear, $350.00 up in unusually large size.

Light gold mohair bear, 12", straw head and torso, cotton stuffed limbs, brown glass eyes, black floss nose and mouth, no claws, leatherized canvas pads, cotton tag sewn into right side seam printed blue: "Hygienic Toys Made in England by the Chad Valley Co. Ltd." Tag adds value. 1930's. $165.00. White long pile mohair dog, 16", all straw, glass eyes, dark brown floss nose, mouth and claws on long feet, shorter pile gold mohair ears, original leather harness. (Author). $135.00.

His handsome square nose presents a pleasant profile to the world. 16", probably English, tan/gold mohair, straw stuffed, black *leather* pads, fully jointed. Black floss nose and mouth, glass eyes, squeaker all enhance his self image, as does his old rayon plaid bow. Courtesy Nan C. Moorehead. $175.00.

Two tagged "Chad Valley" bears: 16½", gold mohair, label on right side, brown coated fabric pads, black floss nose/mouth, glass eyes contribute to a contented tranquil expression. Both are fully jointed, straw stuffed heads, straw/cotton soft stuffed bodies, squeakers. 12" long pile gold mohair on orange fabric base, brown coated fabric pads, label on right foot. Courtesy Nan C. Moorehead. 16" $195.00; 12" $165.00.

Fred, 12", gold mohair, soft stuffed, fully jointed, glass eyes, gold felt pads. He has been with his 11" sister, Minnie, since 1925 and can't bear to be without her. Merry Thought Shops, England, continued the model into late 1940's). Courtesy Dorene Fox. $300.00 matched pair.

144

Kiss blowing bear, 14½", probably English, light blonde long pile mohair, sheared mohair snout and ear lining, straw stuffed, cream felt pads, fully jointed, brown sewn nose and mouth, probably replaced glass eyes. Charming pointed snout seems to be blowing a kiss from the curved, shapely paw. Courtesy Nan C. Moorehead. $150.00-175.00.

Early inset snout, 20" caramel mohair, straw stuffed, fully jointed, original glass eyes, embroidered nose, mouth and claws, stubby feet, felt pads, growler. Excellent workmanship, probably American, circa 1930 when inset snouts were adopted. Courtesy Vera Tiger. $100.00 up this size.

Gold cotton plush 28″ loveable giant, weighs 5 pounds, firmly stuffed with straw, fully jointed, original glass eyes, black embroidered nose, mouth and claws, canvas pads. Note the square cut of snout giving the English pug look. Probably made in Great Britain during 1930. Teddy lured the geese in park by bringing sack of corn. Courtesy Kathy Teske. $195.00 up.

"Grandpa Bear" 18", gold mohair, straw stuffed, fully jointed, glass eyes, floss nose and mouth, elongated body, stubby feet (pads replaced), growler, pointed inset snout. Inset snouts are not popular with the collectors who are willing to pay the high prices. These circa 1930 bears can be bought reasonably. Courtesy Virginia Joy. $100.00-125.00.

White long pile mohair, 17", straw head with oversize ears, soft stuffed torso and limbs, amber glass eyes, black floss nose and mouth, no claws, sheared mohair long snout, velvet pads, squeaker, fully jointed. In beautiful condition. Knickerbocker $125.00. Framed original print; copyright 1934 by Charlotte Becker. Courtesy Nancy Catlin. $25.00.

Left: 14″, long pile gold mohair, straw stuffed head and torso, soft stuffed limbs, short pile snout and feet (like the 1950's Steiff "Teddy Baby"), glass eyes, black floss nose, mouth and three claws, wide head, velvet plus pads, cardboard innersoles. Surprise is "tinkling" music box that operates on gravity. $165.00.

Right: 13″, long pile white mohair, short pile inset snout, soft stuffed, glass eyes, black floss nose, mouth and claws, red embroidered tongue, replaced pads, squeaker, large ears from the 1930's. Courtesy Marlene Wendt. $135.00 up.

"People look up to me" says this 17″ Teddy with long pile gold mohair. Straw head, soft torso, fully jointed, glass eyes, floss nose and expressive mouth, felt pads. Circa 1930. Courtesy Deborah Ritchey $150.00.

When there are no more of the bears before 1912 to be had these late 20's-30's bears will come into their own. Note the gorgeous color of the mohair on this expressive face, 12″, all straw, fully jointed. Courtesy Roberta Viscusi. $175.00.

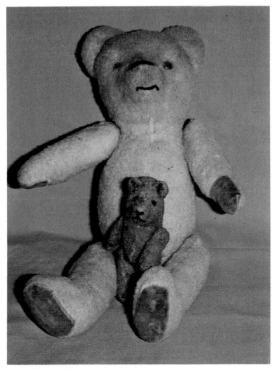

White wool plush, purchased in an Amsterdam antique shop in 1981, 15″, all straw stuffed, glass eyes, applied black velvet nose, embroidered mouth, grey velvet pads, arms and legs attached by strong wire through body (cheaper construction method), rigid head. A self-satisfied expression, both smug and alert. Circa 1930-40. Courtesy Margaret M. Carlson. $135.00.

Serious Farmer Bear: 16″ cinnamon mohair, straw head and limbs, cotton torso, fully jointed, glass eyes, felt pads, floss nose and mouth, squeaker. Note the straight back and serious expression, circa: 1920-30. $225.00. Steiff lamb, 8½″ high black woolly plush, straw stuffed, unjointed, glass eyes, no pads. Red floss nose, mouth, squeaker. Tag "Made in Germany U.S. Zone (1945-52). A rare and large early example of the elusive black lamb. All courtesy Tammie Depew. $125.00 up.

Cinnamon bear: 16″, long pile mohair, all straw, rigid head, jointed limbs, replaced canvas pads on stubby feet, glass eyes, black stitched nose, no claws. Sweet "look." $125.00. Right: 17″ bristle yellow mohair, all straw, football shape torso (1920's), replaced eyes (sometimes replaced eyes enhance the cuteness of a Teddy), long snout, black stitched nose, mouth and claws, felt pads. $175.00. "Friend" is circa: 1915 cotton flannel dog, 9″, shoe button eyes, tan mohair ears, long nose. Courtesy Rosella and Tony Santopietro. $50.00.

White long pile mohair, 17″, straw head, soft stuffed torso and limbs, eyes replaced with *old* buttons, black stitched nose, mouth, no claws, felt pads. Cuddly bear from 1930's. Not uncommon type; more rare in white. Courtesy Rosella and Tony Santopietro. $150.00-175.00.

Little Red Riding Hood: 12″, brown mohair, all straw, unjointed (a transition example of a 30's bear with sewn in place joints), short arms, tin nose (found only in late 1930's). Fun for little girls to dress in doll clothes. Courtesy Marian Swartz. $95.00 up.

Childhood bear of author: 11″ dark brown wool plush, stuffed straw and cotton mix, jointed arms and head, long feet/black felt pads and innersoles, glass eyes, velvet pointed inset snout, velvet front paws, metal nose, embroidered mouth. Note unusual stance on haunches. This 50 year old Teddy is an adaptation of the circus-type. Rare model, but not in demand. (Author). $95.00.

To round out a collection: 22″, very long pile yellow mohair, shaved snout, straw head, soft torso and limbs, glass eyes, velvet pads, black stitched nose, no claws, fully jointed. A huggable Knickerbocker-type from 1930's. Courtesy Diane Hoffman. $125.00.

1930's gold, long pile mohair, 24″, straw head, soft stuffed body, celluloid disc eyes (shank type), shaved mohair inset snout with floss nose, no claws, leather pads, stocky legs. Gund Mfg. Co. favored using these disc eyes. $175.00. Steiff puppies: "Bazi" (Dachshund), 5½″/14cm., No. 1314,0, light brown shaded mohair, jointed neck. 1957-on. $55.00. "Cocker Spaniel" 7½″/19cm., No. 4273/19, red brown mohair, black/white glass eyes, jointed head, circa 1964. $55.00. (Author).

Unusual to find the 1930's tin eyes with decals on an unjointed bear; they are "screwed in" and not easily removeable. Teddy: 14", mohair, lumpy cotton stuffed, velvet pads and ear linings, felt nose replaced. Courtesy Ruth L. Ruder. $35.00.

Purchased in Germany, 21", pink looped wool with texture, straw stuffed, fully jointed, glass eyes, velvet pads, yarn nose and mouth, growler. Unusually thick ears because of bulky material. A child's toy. Circa 1930. Courtesy Ruth L. Ruder. $100.00-200.00.

White cotton plush, 17″, all cotton stuffed, fully jointed, older triangular head shape on a 1930's bear, unusual green glass eyes, stitched nose, *painted* mouth, pink velvet pads. A durable bear which stands out in a collection. This species will become more collectible in the future. $65.00 up.

First edition of paper book: *Moving Pictures Teddies,* 6½″ x 11″, patented Jan. 15, 1907, publisher Ideal Book Builders, Chicago. This popular classic has recently been reprinted in a smaller size by Merrimack Publishing Co., NY. Courtesy Marian Swartz. $45.00

Dachshund: 10″, 1930's cotton plush, leather nose, dressing adds appeal. $50.00. Teddy: 9″, yellow mohair, straw stuffed, glass eyes, brown stitched nose, felt pads; note ear treatment, suggests German import. Courtesy Marian Swartz. $85.00.

9″ beige cotton plush, all soft stuffed, fully jointed, GREEN celluloid disc eyes (shank type), floss nose and mouth, short arms, no pads, velvet foot pads circa 1930. $65.00-75.00 because of unusual qualities. 10″ Sandy, Little Orphan Annies dog, gold cotton plush, soft stuffed inset molded mask face, smiling mouth and cartoon eyes. (Author). $100.00.

Cloth doll 16″, molded mask face, buckram apron and bonnet ruffle, one cotton floss curl, pink calico body/clothes, brown rayon ribbon tie. original price tag: "Ceiling price, $1.19″, WW II. New condition. $25.00. Bear, 16″ wool plush, soft stuffed, celluloid disc eyes/yellow backing (shoe button adaptation), black floss embroidered nose and mouth, red floss tongue, no claws, velvet pads, unusually large head gives variety, fully jointed, sunsuit with two embroidered Teddy Bears that author wore in early 1930's. (Author). $95.00, dressed.

Off white wool plush, 18", all soft stuffed cotton, shiny black button eyes, black floss nose and mouth, white felt pads, no squeaker. Note large head and fat body, fully jointed. Tagged (seldom seen on older Teddy), "Woolnough Co., Inc. NY." Tag adds 30% to value. Original pink and blue ribbon, meant for a new baby gift, circa 1930-40. Courtesy Marlene Wendt. $125.00 with tag.

Bear in sheeps clothing: 13", natural sheepskin, black shoe button eyes, black floss nose and claws, fully jointed (metal discs/springs). Stuffed with wool. Circa 1930's. $85.00; pink bear, 9", glass eyes, $15.00; Younger bear, 12½", tan sheepskin, black embroidered eyes, pink floss nose/mouth, green dyed hide pads and ear linings, wool stuffing, jointed at shoulders and hips. Note short arms. $50.00. Wicker set, $40.00. Courtesy Nan C. Moorehead.

Unusual frosted grey long pile mohair: 13″, straw head, cotton stuffed torso/limbs, brown glass eyes, pink embroidered nose, no claws, felt pads, growler, fully jointed. Longish snout which is the only wear after being loved by owner and her three children. Alert expression. Dates exactly 1939. The beautiful colors in this 1930's period can form a collection in themself. Courtesy original owner, Joyce M. Al-Khafaji. $145.00 up.

Victorian Bruin pull toy: 16″, brown wool plush over paper mache, hollow, nose ring for chain, missing platform on wheels. The very early toys were not jointed. Lifelike. Courtesy Diane Hoffman. $150.00 incomplete.

A work of art: 28″, oversize Steiff (early ear button) bear on cast iron spoked wheels. This spectacular toy stands 20″ tall, thick pile silky light golden mohair, all straw, original shoe button eyes, black stitched nose and mouth, felt pads with long feet (a characteristic of early Steiff animals.) Hole on back for pull-string growler. The silk bow frames the unforgettable face. Circa pre-1908. N.P.A.

Pull toy bear: 22″, dark chocolate brown (almost black), curly long pile mohair, all straw stuffed, glass eyes, felt pads, cast iron spoked wheels painted bronze. German. Courtesy Diane Hoffman. $350.00 up.

161

Riding bear: 21″, rich brown curly mohair, all straw, glass eyes, floss nose and mouth, felt pads, long feet, cast iron spoked wheels. These riding bears have charming faces and were made by many companies both here and in Europe. No Japanese look-alikes are known. (Author). $350.00 up.

Pensive bear on wheels: 13″ high, 19″ long, medium brown thick pile plush, straw stuffed, on cast iron frame and 2½″ wheels. Missing ears cleverly replaced with mouton fur. Ears often missing on riding animals because of being used as handles. Courtesy Rosella and Tony Santopietro. $300.00-350.00.

162

Steiff pull toy, 6½″ high, 9″ long, worsted wool/nap (as often found in the 1910-15 toy era), all straw, unjointed, shoe button eyes, black floss nose, mouth and claws, beige felt pads. "Steiff" imprinted on leather collar, pewter ear button/ff underscored, original pull string, cast iron spoked wheels. (Author). $275.00 up.

"Gulliver", the traveling bear, all set to go on his wheels. 14″ long, heavy wire frame is covered in brown worsted wool/nap, straw stuffed, shoe button eyes, yarn stitched nose and mouth, leather collar, cast iron spoked wheels. Original string attached to nose ring. Circa early 1900's. Courtesy Dorene J. Fox. $350.00.

Riding bear/pull toy on cast iron wheels: 22" long, short cotton plush, straw stuffed, glass eyes, unusual open mouth lined with leather. Seems to smile. Cast iron wheels were not used after the 1920's. Courtesy Marian Swartz. $350.00.

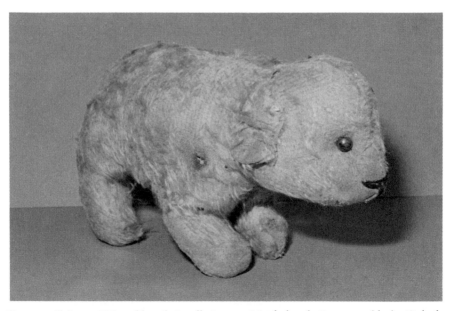

Bear on all fours, 10", gold mohair, all straw, original shoe button eyes, black stitched nose. Early example. Courtesy Beverly L. Krein. $75.00.

Bear on wheels: a child's delight and a collector's dream. Brown cotton plush riding bear, straw stuffed, glass eyes, floss nose/mouth, black rubber tires, disc wheels on heavy red steel frame. $325.00.

Some collectors feel gentle wear to their bears gives added charm. 12", light gold mohair, deep-set shoe button eyes, floss nose, mouth and claws, hump, long snout, curved arms, long slender feet, felt pads. Note child's hankie; Teddy Bear in gay colors is fun to carry, $7.00. Worn Teddy Bear, $175.00. (Author).

1930's brown/gold cotton plush pull toy, 12″ high, straw stuffed head, soft stuffed body, glass eyes on wire, stitched nose and mouth. Note tail that most wheeled bears have, metal frame, black rubber disc wheels. Presents a good historical study of wheeled toys. $95.00.

White mohair Teddy Bear, 9″, button eyes, black stitched nose and mouth, no claws, squeaker, white felt pads. Circa 1930-50. $65.00. Courtesy Nan C. Moorehead.

VI.
Teddy Bears,
1940-1980

Margot Pandel '84

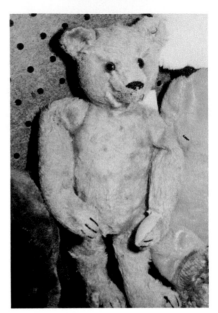

More than lifesize, 6'tall, all mohair and straw, fully jointed, dramatic brown glass eyes enlarged by black felt backing, black hard plastic nose, embroidered claws, felt pads. Used as the campaign manager in a mayorial race. Purported to be a store display from Harrod's Department Store, London. Circa 1930-40. Rare. Courtesy Diane Hoffman. $1,500.00.

1941 Steiff with printed button, ff underscored; 13", light gold mohair, all straw, fully jointed, brown glass eyes, black floss embroidered nose, mouth missing, long snout, felt pads/claws, squeaker. By 1941 the feet and arms were shorter but had not lost the slightly curved paw tapering at the end. This bear has been to Smith college, and loved by the original owner and her four children. Courtesy original owner Kate Denious. In played-with condition, $200.00 up.

Steiff, 19", gold mohair with same length hair over entire face, all straw, glass eyes, black floss nose, mouth and claws, light orange felt pads, very vocal growler, fully jointed, Tagged "Original Teddy". First owner purchased this favorite in early 1940's. Courtesy Diane Hoffman. $250.00-300.00.

Biggies: unusual 32″ early brown cotton plush, solidly cotton stuffed, glass eyes/ brown felt backing, felt nose, sewn on ears, no pads, unjointed. Well made, circa early 1940's. $75.00-95.00 for size.

Light gold standing: 34″, synthetic plush, straw stuffed, glass eyes, floss nose/mouth, felt pads, fully jointed. Circa 1940-50. $85.00

Bright gold, 29″, plush, straw stuffed, fully jointed, shaved snout, stitched nose and mouth, felt pads. Circa early 1940's. $150.00. All courtesy Vera Tiger.

Chad Valley: 26″ in dentist's chair, honey color short pile mohair, straw stuffed head, soft stuffed limbs, straw and kapok torso, glass eyes, embroidered nose and claws, fully jointed, beige muslin pads with tag sewn on left foot: "Hygenic Toys Made in England by Chad Valley". A very desirable and hard-to-find bear in this size. Adds variety and interest to a collection. Courtesy Diane Hoffman. $350.00 up.

Chintz and plush (wartime substitute), 13″, brown/gold cotton plush, sewn on clothes, shoes added. Tagged "Ideal". These models of toys had a limited production. Courtesy Virginia Joy. $45.00.

Wistful expression: 13″, golden orange mohair, soft stuffed, fully jointed, large glass eyes, embroidered nose, mouth and claws, brown felt pads, front paws slightly upturned, voice box. Tags if present are always on foot from "Merry Thought, Ironbridge Shops, Made in England". Post-war production of a continuing style. Courtesy Margaret M. Carlson. $135.00 up.

Gund with tag, 15″, brown mohair, inset nose, hard stuffed cotton head, soft stuffed cotton body, fully jointed, celluloid disc eyes, shank-type, replaced felt pads, floss nose, felt tongue. Excellent quality bear, circa 1940. Courtesy Ruth L. Ruder. $95.00.

Andy Panda, character from 1940, 18″, painted mask face, rubber hands, all original. Book: *Adventures of Andy Panda*, 1940. Hard to find in mint. Courtesy Virginia Joy. Andy Panda, $95.00; book, $15.00.

Left: 18″, black dyed lambswool, soft stuffed, embroidered eyes, longer feet, black stitched nose with white accents, Mickey Mouse-type ears, stocky build, fully jointed. Well-constructed Teddy but will not last due to drying of hide. Fewer black bears sold because facial features do not delineate well, and dark colors are threatening to a child. $75.00.
Cinnamon mohair with hat, 17″, straw head, torso and limbs hard stuffed cotton, glass eyes, velvet pads, fully jointed. Cute expression. Tagged "Knickerbocker", circa 1940-50. Made to last. Courtesy Marian Swartz. $85.00.

Scotch Bearkin: 9" gold mohair, all straw, glass eyes, brown floss nose, squeaker, replaced pads; dressed in original outfit of tartan kilt, red velvet blouse/white collar, pinned on glengarry cap and sporran. Missing red leather shoes. F.A.O. Schwarz' own design as seen in Christmas Catalog, 1938 on. Rare in this outfit. $150.00.
Steiff from late 1940's: 6" honey mohair, same as above but no pads or squeaker. Original yellow bow. $125.00.
Steiff from 1950-55: 8", honey mohair, all straw, glass eyes, dark brown floss nose, mouth and claws, squeaker, fully jointed. $150.00.
1950 Steiff: 3½", honey mohair, all straw, glass bead eyes, long feet, no pads, fully jointed. $85.00 up. All courtesy original owner, Carol Matchett.

Spotted bear: 21", rabbit fur, all straw stuffed, clear glass eyes/dark pupil, black felt heart shaped nose, embroidered red mouth, hide pads, fully jointed. Animal hide from 1940's will not last, it splits at jointing. A decorative bear. Courtesy Diane Hoffman. $125.00.

171

9" beige Steiff, short pile mohair, all straw, brown floss nose/mouth and claws, felt pads. Nicely detailed bear circa 1940-50. $135.00-150.00.
Lamb circa 1890, $15.00. All courtesy Hazel Mathews.

German import: 11", grey/beige long pile woolly plush, shaved muzzle, all straw, fully jointed, glass eyes, flesh color oval felt pads, stitched nose and claws, arms 5" long, legs 5½" long, small hump. Cloth tag on right ear, "Made in U.S. Zone Germany". Has a look of pugnacious scrappiness. Different. Circa 1945-52. Courtesy Linda and Ken Holsworth. $165.00 up.

British Bear: 16", pale gold mohair, straw stuffed, glass eyes, silk floss embroidered nose (unusual), brown felt pads, squeaker, fully jointed. Given new to original owner in England, 1949. Courtesy Pauline M. Davidson. $135.00 up.

172

Cuddly bear: 23″, with an arm span of 19″. Highest quality shaggy synthetic white plush to make him quite unusual. Soft stuffed, sheared plush snout pushed in from years of hugging, black embroidered nose and claws. Eyes are black and amber plastic glued in two layers to give three dimensions. A unique bear of his day (1949). Hard to replace this model. Continues in the company of original owner, Bunny Miller. $55.00 up.

Schuco "Yes/No" Teddy: 21″, long pile pinkish gold curly mohair (splendid color), straw stuffed, clear glass eyes/black pupil, (Schuco often used these clear eyes), black floss nose, mouth and claws, backward front paws, felt pads/cardboard innersoles, tail as lever operates head, growler, fully jointed. Schuco made these mechanical bears from 1926-1950's. They are not hard to find, yet much sought. Every collector wants at least one. This is unusually large size, mint condition from 1948. Courtesy Carol Matchett, original owner. $400.00 up.

Schuco, 13″, "Yes/No" bear, pinkish cast to gold short pile mohair, all straw, clear glass eyes/black pupil, black floss nose, mouth and claws, operate tail to move head. Red chest tag: "Schuco Pat. Pend., Tricky" on front; on back, "U.S. Zone, Germany". A panda "Tricky" was also made in the 1950's. Learn to recognize these distinctive soulful faces. Courtesy Carol Matchett, original owner. $250.00-300.00 up.

Schuco: 22″, pinkish cast to long pile fluffy mohair, all soft stuffed, glass eyes, black floss nose and claws, felt pads/cardboard inner-soles. Tail activates head. The latest version of the ever-popular "Yes/No" Teddy Bear. Courtesy Betty Shelley. $350.00 up.

German: 11″ and 14″ light beige (popular 1950's color) mohair, straw stuffed, fully jointed, glass eyes, floss nose, mouth and claws, felt pads, squeaker. The Teddys appear earlier than they are: superior import quality from 1950's. Early dresser courtesy Virginia Joy. N.P.A. Bears courtesy Vera Tiger. $125.00 and $150.00.

German import: 9″, long pile honey-beige mohair, shaved muzzle, all straw, glass eyes, flesh color round felt pads, embroidered nose, mouth and long claws, fully jointed, small hump, missing ear. (To repair: split good ear and back with felt or velvet.) Arms and legs all 4½″ long. Circa 1950's. Courtesy Linda Holsworth. $75.00.

22″ with a tail, early cotton plush, soft stuffed, orange plastic eyes, black floss nose, short curved arms. Bathing trunks circa 1940 are well fitted to the bear. $25.00-35.00. Woolly plush 8″ carrying bear, unjointed, black metal nose, oil cloth strap and collar. An interesting novelty. $10.00. Courtesy Bev and Tim Murray.

Picnic Bear (seated), 13½″, long pile brown mohair, straw head, torso/limbs soft stuffed, fully jointed, large black button eyes/white felt backing, cream velvet pads and snout, floss nose, mouth and claws. Circa 1940-50. $95.00-125.00.
Teddy Bear pitcher, $5.00.
Standing Bear, 15″, light gold mohair, straw stuffed head, soft torso/limbs, fully jointed, glass eyes, pads woven fabric, embroidered nose, mouth, no claws, growler. Wonderful crooked smile. $175.00. Courtesy Nan C. Moorehead.

Made by "Character". Pink and white thick pile rayon plush, 14", button eyes with white felt backing, black embroidered nose and mouth, unjointed, soft stuffed. Teddy's appearance has changed over the years to be "roly-poly" in the 1950's. This conformation was made over a relatively short time span. One wonders if they will become the most scarce by the year 2000. Courtesy Rosella and Tony Santopietro. $35.00.

Jazz: Bassist, 18", mohair and velvet, soft stuffed, fully jointed, metal discs, hard plastic eyes/black felt backing, cream velvet pads and snout, black felt triangular nose, embroidered mouth. 1940-50. Bass, $15.00; bear, $75.00.
Pianist, 25", 1950's, cream mohair, straw stuffed head, torso/limbs soft stuffed, fully jointed, hard plastic eyes on stem, shaved mohair pads and snout, hard plastic molded nose, embroidered smiling mouth, large head. Has cloth tag "Made in West Germany for Sears, Roebuck & Co." Piano/stool, $45.00; violin, $10.00; bear $85.00.
Drummer, 17½", brown/white cotton plush, 1940's, straw stuffed, glass button eyes, white short plush pads and snout, embroidered nose and claws, felt pads, cardboard innersoles. Note big ears/inner structure of wire, missing left ear covered by old straw hat. Drum $125.00; bear, $85.00. All courtesy Nan C. Moorehead.

Intriguing bear with short pile mohair (long) feet and snout: 10″, long pile gold mohair, straw stuffed, markedly curved long arms, no pads, fully jointed, embroidered nose, open mouth. Post W.W. II. Note: legs set far apart. Courtesy Darlene Zezula. $150.00.

Bear with composure: 13″, Steiff, post-war production, pale gold mohair, straw stuffed, fully jointed, brown glass eyes/black pupil, black floss nose, mouth and claws, beige felt pads, squeaker. Courtesy Wanda Loukides. $300.00.

The popular character "Smokey Bear". As a tribute to the Ideal Toy Corporation's Teddy Bear contribution, the United States government authorized them on their 50th anniversary to make "Smokey the Bear", the symbol of the National Forest Service. Left: the third version 18" plush, tagged "Ideal . . . ", no pull string voice box, black washer grip eyes/felt backing, plastic hat is sewn onto head through two holes. (Author). $35.00.
Center: 18" second version, rayon plush, vinyl molded face, glassene eyes, wears "Smokey" outfit/felt hat, (missing shovel), 1954. (Author). $45.00.
Right: 16" with pull string talking mechanism. He says the cutest things. In working condition, this is the most scarce of the three. (Author). $45.00.

"Smokey", 4¼", hard plastic, jointed head and arms, molded on belt and hat (with name), blue painted pants, missing shovel. Marked: "Tonka, Hong Kong". A seldom seen miniature Smokey. Courtesy Beth Everhart. $5.00.

Original "Punkinheads", tagged "Merry Thought Hygenic Toy Made in England". These special twins are 10", dark gold mohair with lighter chest and inner ears, two-tone white/black pupil glass eyes, black embroidered nose with smiling mouth, unusual long curly white mohair topknot insert. Feet and snout are gold velvet plush, brown felt pads, original felt pants, red and green. Made in many sizes up to 6' exclusively for the T. Eaton Co. of Canada from 1952-59. Characters taken from a fable: if hair was cut it would grow back long overnight. Accessories made with this figure: shirts, slippers, etc. "Cheeky Bear" is a relative of the original "Punkinhead", a great favorite. $150.00 each.

Carmel mohair bear on red wooden wheels: 15" long, 11" high, hard stuffed straw, shoe button eyes, black stitched nose, long feet. Early 1900's. $175.00. All courtesy Marlene Wendt.

1955, large, 22": light gold mohair, straw head, soft torso and limbs, plastic eyes, velvet pads, black embroidered nose, fully jointed. Excellent quality. Courtesy Kirsten Deats. $100.00-150.00.

179

Black high-grade acrylic, 17″, soft stuffed, plastic eyes with felt backing, rigid head, jointed limbs, brown embroidered nose, red felt tongue, yellow acrylic round pads. Circa 1955. Add value for black. Courtesy Carol Matchett. $75.00.

Tagged "Knickerbocker", 14″ gold long pile mohair, soft stuffed, plastic eyes, felt nose, pinwale corduroy snout and pads, chubby, fully jointed. Well-functioning music box, appealing to instincts of childhood. A nice bear to have around. Circa 1950's. Courtesy Carol Matchett. $75.00.

Two American favorites: Left, 19″ orange mohair, straw stuffed, fully jointed, fat round body, glass eyes, shaved mohair inset snout, stitched nose and mouth, no claws, felt tongue, tagged "Gund". Felt tongues on bears of this style typify Gund, Inc., which has been in business since 1898. Because of the high quality many of these bears endure a child's love and can be found today. Right: 17″, thick short pile synthetic plush, straw stuffed, glass stick-pin eyes framed with airbrushing, felt nose and stitched mouth, felt snout and pads, squeaker, fully jointed. The eye treatment (airbrush strokes) and felt inset snout were both used by Knickerbocker. This Teddy would be velvety soft to the child's touch. Courtesy Vera Tiger. $85.00 each.

Lustrous soft white mohair, 9″, straw head, soft torso and limbs, brown glass eyes, tan embroidered nose matching the chamois pads, squeaker, fully jointed. Suggests English origin, Alpha Farnell. Circa 1950. Courtesy Carol Matchett. $65.00.

Reddish-brown mohair, 10″, soft stuffed, fully jointed, glass eyes, black embroidered nose, chamois pads, no claws, original white knit scarf and cap sewn on. Tagged "Alpha Farnell, Made in England" with ears sewn laterally as typical of that company. Circa 1955-60. Courtesy Carol Matchett. $65.00.

Cuddly twins with collector appeal: 15″, 14″, 1950's synthetic plush, soft stuffed, unjointed, no pads, glass eyes with felt backing, black cotton pompom nose, floss embroidered mouth. Tagged: "Master Industries, St. Paul, Minn." (Author). $30.00-35.00.

Rick Mandel at six weeks of age with first Teddy, and bear today. 10″ cotton plush, soft stuffed head and limbs, cotton lined zippered torso, plastic eyes (one of which child swallowed), tagged "Teddy Kuddles, Knickerbocker Toy Co." 1957. Of sentimental value only. (Author).

"Teddy Baby" one of the all-time favorites, 11″ (also came in 3½″, 8½″ and 16″ sizes), long pile brown mohair, beige short mohair snout and feet, all straw, fully jointed, open felt mouth, brown glass eyes, black floss nose and claws. Leg stance compares to an actual bear cub. Shown in 1957 Steiff catalogue. Leather collar and ear button. Needed to complete a Teddy Bear collection. Courtesy Rosella and Tony Santopietro. $250.00 up.

Left: Shaggy dark brown mohair, 15″, soft filled, inset snout, stitched nose, white felt pads, sewn on ears, fully jointed. Circa 1930's. $125.00.
9″ Steiff with short legs. Older. $60.00.
The elusive and sought after "Teddy Baby", 11″/28 cm. No. 7328,2. Steiff ear button and collar, honey mohair, straw stuffed, fully jointed, glass eyes, open mouth. $300.00.
Quilt with Teddies appliqued by owner. All courtesy Vera Tiger.

A stunning assembly of scarce and amusing German open mouth bears. Largest: 21″, tagged "Grisly" on pin embedded in chest. Long pile honey mohair, soft stuffed, glass eyes, mohair pads (unusual), fully jointed. Note the unusual mouth treatment. German, 1950's. $175.00 up.
9″ caramel/white chest "Zotty". $95.00.
8″ Steiff mohair "Panda", $150.00.
15″ open mouth, gold frosted mohair, Steiff "Zotty", $150.00.
11″ Steiff "Cosy Teddy", dark brown/white chest, $95.00.
10″ gold frosted mohair Hermann (no chest plate and distinctive nose), $85.00.
All courtesy Vera Tiger.

Steiff Panda Bear: 8½″/22 cm. No. 5322,2, white/black mohair, fully jointed, brown glass eyes, squeaker, black floss nose, open felt mouth, suedine pads/cardboard innersoles. Jointed mohair pandas are scarce. Bought in Germany in 1965. Courtesy Tim Murray. $150.00-200.00.

Panda: 9″ rayon plush, all straw, ears sliced in (Japan), googly glass eyes, flannel snout, interesting disproportion of large head, squeaker. A novelty from 1950's. Courtesy Marian Swartz. $35.00.

Panda, 12″, textured rayon body, thin plastic molded/painted face, vinyl lined ears, soft stuffed. Possible carnival toy adapted from a cartoon character (pie-shaped eyes). 1950's. Courtesy Carolyn Altfather. $15.00-20.00.

Steiff Panda: 13″, dralon and cotton plush, soft stuffed, fully jointed, brown glass eyes, open jersey mouth and pads, airbrushed tongue, black twisted floss nose, no claws. Ear button is incised (not raised) script. Rare. Courtesy Susan Roeder. $200.00-250.00.

Trio. Left: 12″, black and white cotton plush, straw stuffed head, soft stuffed body, un-jointed, replaced eyes, metal nose and floss mouth. Typical moon-faced Panda. Circa 1930's. (Author). $50.00-65.00.

Center: 9″, thick rayon plush, seated, unjointed, all straw, black stitched mouth, brown glass eyes, long legs, sewn on ears. Made to hold radio just as several decades earlier bears held music boxes. Rayon tag sewn into seam, "Made in Taiwan". Circa 1960's. (Author). $45.00.

Right: 13″, acrylic plush, stuffed with acrylic shredded clippings, plastic eyes, yarn nose and mouth, fully jointed, tagged "Commonwealth Toy Co., Made in Korea". (Author). $15.00.

Bear cousin: "Koala Bear", 5"/12 cm., No. 12K/4312, begging, mohair, grey felt nose and feet, stitched fingers/separate thumb, glass eyes, jointed head only, all straw stuffed. Hard to find. Circa 1957-on. Courtesy Susan Roeder. $55.00.

Steiff "Zotty", 11", platinum frosted mohair, lighter chest, soft stuffed, glass eyes, embroidered nose and claws, felt pads and open felt mouth, fully jointed. In 1979 the fur color became darker. Courtesy Rosella and Tony Santopietro. $125.00.

German giant: 25", gold and brown frosted shaggy mohair. "ELI/puppen und Spieltiere" often used variegated furs. Straw stuffed, fully jointed, long inset mohair snout, glass eyes, embroidered features, sewn on ears, felt pads. "BEAR" blocks are a fun accessory for this child-size bear. Circa 1950's. Courtesy Vera Tiger. $150.00-175.00.

14" grey/beige curly wool plush, rayon plush snout, all straw, black floss nose, mouth and claws, plastic eyes, fully jointed, felt pads. Attractive, but Japan-import quality. $45.00. 5" Japanese, rigid neck, sparse gold mohair, ears sliced in. Circa 1933. $15.00. All courtesy Bev Murray.

1950's revival: 18", frosted woolly plush, sheared rayon plush snout, all straw, rigid head, arms jointed with rod to move in unison, ears sliced into head, (probably Japanese), plastic nose on long snout, embroidered mouth, round felt pads, growler. Very photogenic. Courtesy Rosella and Tony Santopietro. $50.00-65.00.

Teddy riding horse: 6" blonde mohair, all straw, brown floss nose and mouth, glass eyes, well contoured legs and long feet. $95.00-$125.00.
In cart: 11" excellent quality made by "Character", beige mohair, soft stuffed, plastic eyes, airbrushed claws, felt pads, fully jointed. Note round head. Bear for a child, circa 1960. Courtesy Marian Swartz. $35.00.

Steiff with F.A.O. Schwarz yellow plastic tag: 18″ beige mohair, straw stuffed, shaved muzzle, glass eyes, prong ear button, felt pads. Purchased in early 1960's. Rabbit arm puppet, 15″, circa 1978. Courtesy David Parrish. Bear, $125.00.

"Floppy Zotty", 11″/28 cm. No. 85/12/7328, 6½″/17 cm. No., 85/12/7317, earlier platinum color frosted mohair, soft and cuddly, eyes embroidered as in sleep over brown felt, brown floss nose, claws airbrushed onto felt pads, open felt mouth. Since a popular child's toy, hard to find in mint condition. 1957-1971. Chest tag and ear button. Large, $85.00; small, $55.00.
Hand puppet (Teddy), 6½″/17 cm. No. 12/317, long brown mohair, shaved mohair snout, open felt mouth/pink shading, glass eyes. $25.00.
This hand bear dates from 1969; however, still available with little change. $25.00.
All courtesy Susan Roeder.

China feeding dish, 7½″ diam. Marked "A.M. Milne, Winnie the Pooh, Made in Germany, Richard G. Kreuger, N.Y., Stephen Slesinger, Inc." This scarce dish depicts a segment of the story where Eeyore loses his tail. Circa 1931. $65.00.
10″ official Disney version tagged: "Winnie the Pooh, Walt Disney Productions, Gund Mfg. Co., Made in Japan." Original stocking cap and sweater. Mid-1960's. $50.00-65.00. Both courtesy Beth Everhart.

Polar Bear: 13″, cream color mohair, airbrush markings claws and ears, straw filled, glass eyes, embroidered nose and mouth, shaved mohair snout and feet, tail. Airbrushing technique flourished in 1960's. Note the positioning of arms typifying "Anker", a German manufacturer of quality toys, along with Grisly and Clemens. Courtesy Vera Tiger. $95.00.

188

Tagged "Anker/Munich", 22", wool plush, straw stuffed, embroidered nose, mouth and claws, glass eyes, felt pads on nice large feet, fully jointed. Finest German import quality. Circa 1960's. Courtesy Kay Bransky. $150.00.

Christmas bear: 14" acrylic plush, all soft stuffed, jersey knit nightclothes made to body, sewn on hat, felt backed black plastic eyes, red felt nose. Colorful. Circa 1960's. Courtesy Rosella and Tony Santopietro. $25.00.

189

A child's bear from the 1950-60's: curly cotton plush, 18″, soft stuffed, unjointed, curved arms, no pads, effective black/white cotton pompom eyes, black pompom nose, red felt tongue, pointy snout. Tagged: "Bijou Toys Inc. . . New York, a Bijou Boutique." Rayon scarf added. (Author). $40.00.

Perky example of a 1950-60's "new thrust" bear, 14½″, sitting, tri-color synthetic plush, labeled "It's a Wonderful Toy made in USA by IDEAL." Brown pompom eyes, felt nose, white plush paws. Stuffed with old grey cotton and wools. Courtesy Nan C. Moorehead. $25.00.

"Gentle Ben", a prime time TV star, 17″ synthetic plush, soft stuffed, unjointed wonder. Plastic disc eyes, brown felt eyelashes, plastic nose, open shocking pink felt mouth, red felt tongue to side, original silver link collar. Tagged: "Mattell... Gentle Ben, 1967". An innovative pull string bear that speaks five phrases: "I'll protect you and keep you safe from harm", "I think it's time for my long winters nap", "I can pull a wagon real good", "Here I am, your faithful pal, Gentle Ben", and "Hold me close and give me a bear hug". In 1969, reissued in brown as "Buzzy Bear" for Sears. "Ben" hard to find in working condition. (Author). $55.00.

Knickerbocker can almost always be relied upon for quality products. Four bears circa 1960, 18″ red plush, plastic eyes felt backing, upturned snout, cotton pompom nose, red felt tongue. Beige, blue and gold, 14″, glued on felt noses with smiling watermelon mouths. Cheerful. (Author). $15.00-20.00 each.

"Petsy", 12″/30 cm. Steiff-made 1971-77. Gold dralon, soft stuffed, replaced button eyes, floss nose/mouth, felt pads feet only. Fully jointed, better to iron and sew. Ironing board and iron courtesy Nancy Lucas. Bear courtesy Virginia Joy. $95.00 up.

191

Steiff 26″/66 cm. No. 2021, honey color mohair discontinued in this size (1977). All straw, glass eyes, floss nose and mouth, no claws, short legs, felt pads, shaved muzzle, growler. Old Tag: "Original Teddy". Original red silk ribbon (2″), woven edges. Ready for Christmas morning. (Author). $225.00.

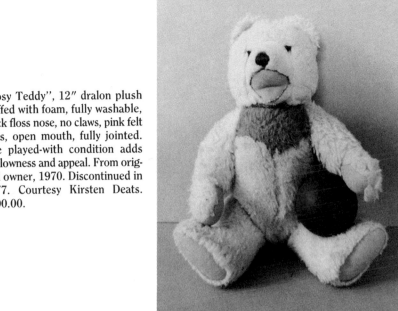

"Cosy Teddy", 12″ dralon plush stuffed with foam, fully washable, black floss nose, no claws, pink felt pads, open mouth, fully jointed. The played-with condition adds mellowness and appeal. From original owner, 1970. Discontinued in 1977. Courtesy Kirsten Deats. $100.00.

German open mouth cuddly bear made by Hermann, (est. 1911). This Zotty-type can be identified by nose embroidery, *yarn* not floss, with straight stitch extending downward either side. No chest plate, 10″, platinum frosted long pile mohair, soft stuffed, open felt mouth, glass eyes, felt pads, black stitched claws, brown nose, squeaker, fully jointed. $85.00.
"Cosy Teddy", 7½″/20 cm., No. 4762/20, caramel color plush (80% dralon, 20% cotton), white chestplate, soft stuffed, brown glass eyes, brown floss nose, no claws, open felt mouth and pads, fully jointed. 1973. Discontinued 1977. Courtesy Susan Roeder. $75.00.

Standing bear left: 5"/12 cm., No. 1445/12, "Browny", fully washable dralon (paper tag), soft stuffed, red suede collar, brown jersey pads. Made in Austria. 1978. C.S.P. Right: 7"/20 cm. No. 6620, "Cosy Orsi", fully washable dralon (large round tag), soft stuffed, open mouth, brown stitched nose, pink felt pads. Old Steiff chest tag. Modern standing bears are not as popular as jointed Teddies. Courtesy Susan Roeder. $65.00.

Wooden bear, 16", original by Rosemary Valpi, peg jointed arms and legs of ¾" wood, head and body of 1½" wood, natural finish. Note that the wood grain gives an appealing body texture. $20.00.

Tagged, "Fontanals Barcelona", written in Spanish, 13", synthetic plush, fully jointed, black hard plastic shank-type eyes, inset snout, squeaker. Of special interest is the use of native materials in the orange raffia embroidered nose, mouth and claws. Courtesy Nan C. Moorehead. $25.00.35.00

194

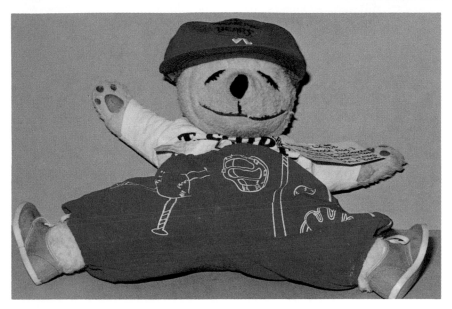

Black bias tape smile: 17″, white synthetic plush, shredded polyurethane, black felt eyelashes only (appearance of sleeping), white felt pads and leather digits, black felt/yarn nose, no voice box. Tagged "Knickerbocker Toy Co. 'The Sleepy Bears' copyright 1977". The imaginative dressing of this bear sets it apart: Generic Bear printed on cap. Goes by name of "Bashful". The legs are manufactured to be spread-eagle style. Courtesy of Tonja Hoopes. $25.00.

Lamb's fleece, 13″, white and dyed black, embroidered eyes and nose. A colorful and imaginative child's bear of exceptional quality. Cost $35.00 in 1976. Courtesy Susan Bowles. $50.00.

Peggy Nisbet bear issued in 1977 to commemorate the Queen's Silver Jubilee. 13″, brown plush, soft stuffed, tan pads, plastic eyes and yarn nose made by a specialist called a "Noser". Tag on foot reads: "Nisbet Childhood Classics by Peggy Nisbet Ltd., Weston, Super Mare, England". Attached is cardboard tag with cleaning instructions. Courtesy Dorene J. Fox. $75.00.

Booklet, "Your Very Special Friend Chan", gold synthetic plush, soft stuffed, plastic eyes, plush nose, floss mouth. Animal Fair, Inc. limited production. Sold for $6.95 in 1977. (Author). $20.00.

Elizabeth Bear-et Browning, 19″, white synthetic plush, polyester fiber filled, non-jointed, closed eyes, thick eye lashes, round plush brown nose, smiling red embroidered mouth. Bows on her toes, gingham dress and bonnet. This bear is for children as well as an adult collector. Limited production by Ms. Noah, Holly Hill, S.C. in 1978. Courtesy Nanci Burney. $50.00.

Amelia Bear-heart, 18″, and airplane 32″, beige synthetic fur, polyester fiber filled, un-jointed, closed eyes, thick eyebrows, round plush nose, pilot's hat with cut out for ears. "Amelia Bear-heart lives! She lives where dreams live, and hope, and moon beams. Her destination: she is flying straight into the arms of a true and loving friend." Limited production by Ms. Noah, Holly Hill, S.C. in 1978. Airplane makes bear of interest. Courtesy Nanci Burney. $85.00.

Advertising Bears are a category in themselves. These somewhat obscure Teddies are from 1970's. "Burgers" and "Sleepy" from Travelodge Motel. Courtesy Virginia Joy. $15.00 each.

Floppy Bear, 36″ nose to rump, tagged "FECO Made in Germany". Thick plush brown undercoat, long silvery guard hairs (true to nature). Soft stuffed, fits anywhere, large two-tone plastic eyes, plush nose, floss mouth, sheared plush muzzle, tail. Highest quality, 1977. Discontinued. (Author). $150.00.

Handmade toys, popular since the beginning of time. materials include: white rabbit fur, mink, crochet yarn and porcelain. Of special interest: the black bear made from a velvet coat (circa 1930), shoe button eyes; "Just-Me" bisque repro doll dressed as a Teddy Bear. Courtesy of Virginia Joy, Vera Tiger and Darlene Zezula. N.P.A.

VII.
Contemporary
Teddy Bears

Mechanical store display from 1980. 42", brown synthetic fur, stuffed with cotton and newspaper, gold plush and painted face, vinyl nose, large plastic eyes, open mouth. Feet are attached to wooden platform with metal and cardboard cannister, when electrified turns head from side to side and waves one arm. One of a kind. Courtesy Marlene Wendt. $300.00 up.

Misha of Moscow fame. Unusual find is a 1930's copy of "Misha, the Little Brown Bear", written and illustrated by Countess Adrienne Segur of Paris, France. $25.00 up.
Soldier, W.W. I, 11" composition and cloth. N.P.A.
NOTE: the 1980 commemorative "Misha" issued only in the Soviet Union for the Russian market was fully jointed and bore no resemblance to the Dakin version. All courtesy Virginia Joy.

200

Misha bears, made in 6", 12", 18" and 24" sizes by R. Dakin & Co. as the official mascot of the 1980 Moscow Olympic Games. A portion of the purchase price of Misha™ went to the support of the Olympic Committee. Dark brown plush with beige ears and snout, filled with shredded clipping and ground nutshells. Large bears: felt eyes and noses; small bears: plastic eyes and noses. Must have Olympic belt to be the original issue. The various sizes make a striking group. Courtesy Nanci Burney. $1.00 per inch at this time.

"Hermann" bear: 36" tall, golden mohair, straw stuffed, embroidered nose and mouth, no claws, hump, fulled jointed, tagged. Ideal proportions in an impressive large size. A special edition with less than 300 made worldwide. Courtesy Kay Bransky. $600.00-800.00.

Bears are hard to fit because of shoulder span and large arm hole size. Baby clothes are best. This Steiff "Molly Bear" is just right to display the owner's baby clothes. Not every bear is entitled to wear this luxury antique dress, coat and bonnet. Courtesy Bev Murray. N.P.A.

1980 Steiff Limited Edition Papa Bear: 5,000 made for export to U.S., 6,000 made for West Germany. With the certificate in English, $350.00 up; with certificate in German, $450.00 up. Mama and Baby, 1981 Limited Edition, $250.00 up. Of the various limited editions since, only these first two have the potential for greatest appreciation. (Author).

Artist Bears are fun to collect and enjoy. There is some investment potential if they are of highest quality, signed and limited. Numbered top to bottom, left to right: No. 1, 3, 6, 7, and 9 by Flore Emory; No. 2 and 10 by James and Linda Spiegel, "Bearly There"; No. 8 and 11 by Veneta Smith, all of Los Angeles County. No. 5 and 11 (far left) are old bears, together with a cluster of miniature Steiff animals. All courtesy Deborah Ritchey. Artist Bears average $75.00 up.

"Debonair Bear", Xavier Robert's "movie bear" from his book; hand signed and numbered limited edition of 1000; 26" thick black plush, soft sculpture of pink jersey, firm synthetic stuffing, unusual plastic coated eyes (available in blue and the rarer brown); elegantly attired in a white cotton collar and cuffs with black satin bow tie. An artistic creation for children of all ages. Issue price, 1982: $75.00. Skyrocketing to $125.00 up. "Cabbage Patch Kid," 17", vinyl bald head/freckles, mass produced by Coleco, 1983. Note outfit with the ever popular Teddy Bear applique. Hardest to find are: blacks, bald head, afro hair, freckles, boys and pacifier. Courtesy My Favorite Dolls Shop, Denver, Colorado. CSP.

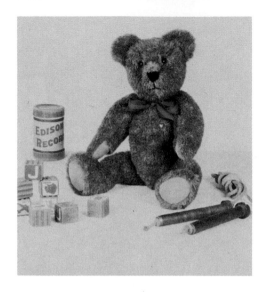

"A Bear With a Heart", 18", unusual *vintage* grey fur (approximately 40-45 years old - acrylic), polyester fiber fill and new cotton clippings, fully jointed (imported hardboard discs), ultra suede pads, embroidered nose, mouth; hump. Number 60/500. Creator and owner, Diane Gard, Fort Collins, Colorado. $100.00.

Bellhop Bear by Sue Kruse, Ltd. Ed. 4/82, 11", synthetic gold plush, felt sewn on clothes, hard stuffed cotton, black shoe button-type eyes, black yarn embroidered nose and mouth, three claws, gold felt pads with cardboard innersoles. Innovative design with an upturned snout, fulled jointed. Tag sewn into back seam. Courtesy Patricia R. Smith. $100.00.

Brown Baby Boy: 18", limited edition Ocala Cub, 229/250 made by Dorothy Bordeaux, Ocala, Florida. 1983. Variegated dark brown (guard hair) acrylic fur, glass eyes, black embroidered nose, brown felt pads, growler, fully jointed. Courtesy Nanci Schroeder. $100.00.

Older white wool plush Artist Bear: 20″, hard stuffed cotton, shoe button eyes, black embroidered upturned nose gives character, fully jointed, Mickey Mouse ears, leather pads, original dress. 1960. $100.00.
Rabbits fit well into scenes. Steiff "Running Rabbit" $45.00; Steiff sitting rabbit, jointed at neck, $45.00. All courtesy Shirlee Glass.

205

"Shirley-o-Bear", original design by Marlene Wendt: 12", gold plush, tan velour pads, blue nylon dress/white dots, white felt shoes. Note the many blonde Shirley Temple curls. $75.00.

Artist's bear: 16", bisque face and feet, painted Mary Jane shoes, acrylic fur body, polyester stuffed, jointed limbs, stationary head. Navy wool sailor jacket, red satin bow. No. 8/10 by Odaca artist Terol Reed. A sensational Teddy. Courtesy Betty Shelley. $200.00.

THE END

Bear *rug*, commercially made, 38", two-tone beige synthetic plush, loosely stuffed with cotton, plastic eyes, pads on back feet only, long 5" snout and no chin. Excellent quality. Manufacturer unknown. Courtesy Vera Tiger. $95.00 up.

VIII.
Teddy Bear
Related Items

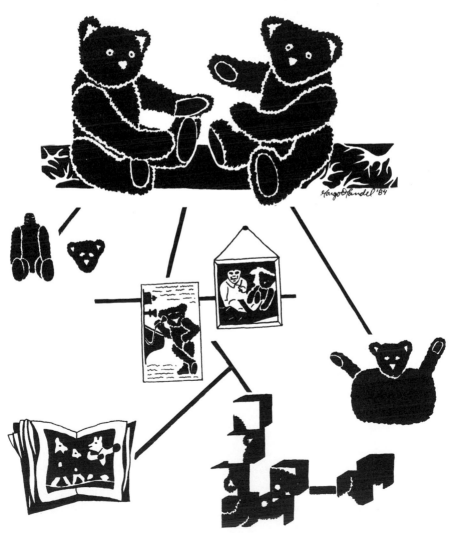

19th century European mechanical: 12″ tall sitting in honey bear fashion, hollow paper mache body covered with brown woolly fur, arms in cradle position, cardboard pads. Head has moving glass eyes which googly up and down when head moves upon a system of lead weights. All activated by a clockwork mechanism. With some wear, $650.00 up.

Avon Teddy Bear perfume bottles. Left is 3″ tall with gold head and collar, more recent than the flocked glass bottle, circa 1978, which is 3½″ tall. (Author). $15.00 each.

Perfume Bottle Bear: 5″, dark gold mohair, metal form inside, fully jointed, head lifts off to reveal a cylindrical glass bottle/stopper. Black painted (worn) metal eyes, no pads, black thread nose and mouth. Early bear, very cute in his own right. These were available in such exotic colors as lavenders, pinks, blue and emerald green. Sold as a novelty in early 1900's. Courtesy Wanda Loukides. $250.00.

209

Santa Clara Bear, 4¼″, black on black pottery, suggestive of a Teddy Bear to someone inclined to think so. Bear lore is prevalent among the Indians of Santa Clara Pueblo. Note the long flowing lines of the miniature. It fits well into a bear collection. Courtesy Carolyn Altfather. $60.00.

Teddy Bear muff dated 1927: 9″ white mohair, unjointed straw stuffed head, brown embroidered nose and claws (feet only), glass eyes, felt pads, soft stuffed muff is lined with white rayon. Professionally dressed by Betty A. Kremp. Sits on a cup stand for display. Desirable. Courtesy Rosella and Tony Santopietro. $250.00.

Embroidery, 19″ x 17″, color printed pattern on sateen canvas. Before 1920. Rare. Courtesy Marian Swartz. $250.00.

Lithograph blocks, 6½"x10", autobus with Teddy Bears, made in Germany, early 1900's. Puzzle makes six pictures. Courtesy Floyd Lillard. $150.00 up.

Teddy Bear muff circa 1930, 10½" high x 8" wide, pink and blue plush, head straw stuffed, muff cotton filled, unjointed head, glass eyes, black floss nose. A treasure from a little girl's past. Courtesy Tammie Depew. $175.00 up.

Cinnamon cotton plush child's muff: 12", soft stuffed, celluloid disc eyes (shank type), black embroidered nose and mouth, no claws, dangly legs are 3" long, muff is lined in velvet. These muffs were made by many companies including Steiff. 1938 exactly. Courtesy Barbara J. Farinsky. $135.00.

Original oil painting by German master, 30″ x 24″. Reclining nude with Teddy Bear (appears to be Steiff). Circa 1908-1910 period; this was a popular style. (Author). N.P.A.

Oil painted photograph, 14″x16″, girl with white Teddy Bear. Circa 1910. Courtesy Marlene Wendt. $150.00 up.

Studio bear used as a *prop* by photographer in 1935. Marlene Wendt at age one. Note that many of the Teddy Bears seen in antique photos did not belong to the child. This bear is a pin jointed, inexpensive, 1930's example. A nice vintage studio portrait with toys. $15.00.

Child's complete service: bowl, plate, cup and saucer. Porcelain with decals of Roosevelt Bears at sports. Mark B&S/crown, Austria. Early 1900's. Rare in mint condition. Courtesy Virginia Lillard. $200.00.

Ceramic feeding dish, 7¼″ diam., made for International Silver Co. "I go here says the fork, I go here says the spoon," in gold leaf. Easy to find. Circa late 1930's. (Author). $25.00.

Toboggan Teddies soap: toboggan 7″, soaps 3″. White castile molded soaps, red flannel scarves, eyes and nose painted brown. Red cardboard toboggan marked: "Toboggan Teddies, Castile Soap, Modeled by Lightfoot, New York". The chances of this 1947 set surviving complete and mint are very slim because disposable items become the most rare. These colorful replicas fall into the category of "functional art", along with perfume bottles and Teddy Bear compacts. Since the figures are sitting in their sled (nest egg fashion), the value is more than tripled. Courtesy Patricia R. Smith. $95.00.

Tomato can: 4½″, "Bear Brand California Canneries, San Francisco, California", circa 1906-16. This has a dual purpose as a colcible: old advertising tin or Teddy Bear related item. Rare: the common is the most easily discarded. Courtesy Marian Swartz. $45.00.

Postcards: many adapted from children's books. 2nd row center: rhyme corresponds with the various colors that the Teddy can be embroidered (rare). Different examples can be collected in sets, are fun to search for and take up little room. Condition is of prime importance with any ephemera. Courtesy Diane Hoffman. Mint condition: $8.00-10.00 each.

Roosevelt Bear-type Inkwell: 7½″, open mouth/teeth, glass eyes, hinged at neck. Carved wood. For the collector who prefers a more life-like bear copy. Courtesy Marian Swartz. $85.00.

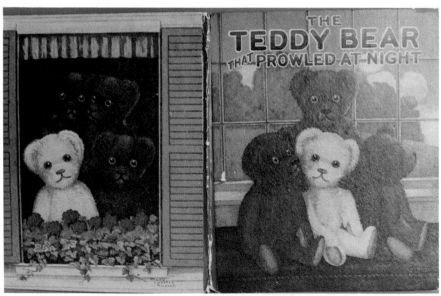

"The Teddy Bear that Prowled at Night", Sam'l Gabriel Sons & Co., New York, 1924. First edition. There are famous bears roaming through children's books: Pooh, Paddington and Corduroy. New bears such as Wilberforce are appearing to tell happy stories. Courtesy Marian Swartz. $65.00.

IX.
Steiff Dolls

Monkey Man, comical policeman; 17", extraordinary figure, fully jointed, felt face with seam to nose, felt ears and hands, muslin torso and legs, striking copper color mohair fur, navy blue felt jacket sewn to arms (closure with blank metal buttons), cotton plaid trousers, beautifully crafted leather boots with nail holes for standing, pewter ear button/ff underscored. Note his official bearing. A perfect artistic representation of the master toymaker's craft. $900.00. Accompanied by 11" "Yes/No" Bellhop monkey, $250.00; Steiff white fully jointed chimpanzee, $45.00; 4½" Steiff "Coco", $45.00.

Steiff character: 18", fully jointed, all felt, seam down center face, shoe button eyes, painted features, bulb nose and big ears. The shoes (with intricate leatherwork) enable the doll to be self supporting. Green felt jacket, red/white cotton knit shirt, red/white check cotton flannel pants, early pewter ear button. An important doll for the historical record as well as for its aesthetic merits. N.P.A.

Accessories are valuable complements to a collection. Shoenhut duck; Steiff cat on cast iron wheels, yellow glass eyes, early ear button, $300.00.

Ichabod, the tranquil German school teacher, 18"/36 cm., ear button, beige felt, carton body, pin jointed arms, legs swing on torso with discs, black glass eyes, one face seam down middle, blonde mohair wig on wig base, dressed in made-to-body black felt suit (coat tail and lapels are separate loose pieces), black leather pointed shoes sewn to feet, black covered thin legs, black silk cravat, black felt sewn-on hat, schoolbag. Circa 1905-11. Courtesy Evelyn Krause. $850.00-900.00.

One of the characters that won grand prize at St. Louis, 1904, and Brussels, 1910. Shown in display lifting a young child. 21½", ear button, all beige felt carton body, fully jointed, black glass eyes, blonde mohair rooted hair, four face seams, slight smile. Dressed in jodhpurs, fitted coat, striped shirt, strap belt, knee-to-ankle leggings, missing tam-type hat, special laced and removeable shoes. Besides representing the true German, this is the type of doll of which one never tires. Courtesy Evelyn Krause. $900.00

Unusually large German character, 22", ear button, beige felt carton body, fully jointed, hinged knees, amber glass eyes/black pupil, center face seam, one mouth seam, carrot mohair wig inset into skull, large flap ears, special smile being pleased with his station in life. Striped cotton removeable pant, grey wool coat made to doll, four decorative buttons, red shoulder cords. Removeable black leather boots with 14 Steiff buttons. (See detail). Courtesy Evelyn Krause. $900.00.

To add variety to the German scene: an *unwigged* doll, 18″, identified by having 14 Steiff buttons on shoe soles, beige felt carton body, pin jointed arms, disc jointed legs and neck, hinged knees, black glass eyes, one face seam down middle, ears stitched in complete detail, hair outlined with a cover of dark flocking, center face seam makes center part in hair. Official's suit: brown/tan removeable pants, navy coat with flare made to body, buttons on cuffs, braid on shoulder seam, double leather belt with buckles and metal rings (three metal rings and leather straps add interest to back). Special removeable boots with Steiff studs. Gloved hands, not removeable. This absolutely successful doll has a youthful appearance. Courtesy Evelyn Krause. $900.00.

German postal carrier with dignity of occupation, 19″, button in ear, beige felt carton body, pin jointed arms, disc jointed head and legs, hinged knees, amber glass "Teddy Bear eyes", one face seam, carrot red mohair moustache, wonderful profile. Dressed in brown/green plaid loosely fitting pants, navy felt fitted coat made to body, (flare to coat is a separate piece at hip), five metal coat buttons similar to a Teddy Bear's blank ear button, gold and navy arm band, red shoulder braid, gloves made on to cupped hands, loose removeable black leather boots with 14 Steiff buttons (nail heads) on each sole. Circa 1910. Courtesy Evelyn Krause. $900.00.

221

Inspection Sargeant: 21″, felt face with center seam, shoe button eyes, fully jointed, hinged knees. Dressed in white linen pants, navy blue felt jacket with red trim and gold buttons, leather belt with a metal buckle. The detail and workmanship would be difficult to duplicate today. Courtesy Ursula Schink. $900.00.

Steiff girl: 14″, all felt, seam down center face, fully jointed, shoe button eyes, painted features with delicate blushing of cheeks, wispy mohair wig, all original in cotton undies and slip, white cotton blouse, red felt laced vest and skirt with black braid trim, red felt pillbox hat/black braid trim, cotton ribbed socks, red felt shoes. Button in ear. A hint of a smile on this pristine example of a unique portrait child. In 1976-77 this doll would have sold for $125.00. Now, $600.00 up.

Hard-to-find early Steiff miniature 3¼″ Teddy Bear with pewter ear button.

From the 1909 production line: girl and boy pair, 11", all felt, seam down center face, fully jointed, shoe button eyes, painted features, delicate blushing of cheeks, wispy mohair wigs. All original. Girl is wearing red knit sweater with matching cap, navy wool flannel skirt, navy wool knit long pants over legs wrapped with navy felt, missing shoes show Steiff foot construction. Boy, "Hubertus": red knit sweater, tan felt hat, brown felt trousers, tan felt puttees with tiny metal "Steiff" buttons, black felt shoes. Leather belt completes the outfit. There is an aura of agelessness about these dolls that cannot be denied. Scarce matched pairs add value. $900.00 up for pair.

Steiff bird, "Bluebonnet": 5", mohair, straw, felt brush-like tail and wings, metal feet. 1957 on. $55.00.

Steiff beauty: 11", all felt with seam down the middle of face, straw stuffed, fully jointed, tiny black glass eyes, smiling painted mouth. Note the stark white-blonde mohair is a bit mussed as in so many of these treasures. This hair was entirely satisfactory because it was impossible for a little girl to pull out. Courtesy Rosemary Moran. $400.00.

Early character: 12"/30 cm. Leprechaun, precursor to later Dwarfs. All felt, straw stuffed, fully jointed, mask shape felt face/seam down middle, comical features, upturned nose, painted wide smiling mouth, inset green glass eyes, stitched ears, applied red mohair beard and brows (bald head), stitched fingers, oversize feet/well made clogs with wooden soles and nails, enabling doll to be free-standing; original costume of orange felt cap and trousers, green vest/belt, carries a velvet and die-cut shamrock with a felt boutonniere, glass beads in center. Delightful early Steiff with ear button/ff underscored in mint condition. Circa 1911. Courtesy Teri Dage. $500.00.

Steiff Girl: 11", felt face seam down the middle and lateral seam to eyes, straw stuffed, fully jointed felt body, blue glass eyes, white mohair wig, stitched mouth (unusual) with pink painting; original clothes of white cotton undies, flannel petticoat, dark grey striped flannel skirt, white cotton blouse, black felt middy, green felt hat. Circa 1910-20. Steiff Chow Dog pull toy: 6½" tall, 8" long, tan mohair and felt, three piece felt face and legs, black shoe button eyes, painted nose, tail stitched to body, straw stuffed, cast iron spoked wheels. Rare 1910-20 toy, mint condition. Courtesy Susan Passarelli. Doll, $550.00 up; dog, $275.00.

Tea Cosey: 17", felt head with seam down the middle, felt shoulderplate, applied ears, glass eyes, large painted "character" mouth, exaggerated nose emphasized by black glasses, detailed felt hands. Dressed in flannel and wool to insulate the teapot. Similar style, but smaller, constructed as hand puppets. Courtesy Brian Dorian. $500.00.

Steiff doll: 16", felt with seam down center face, original shoe button eyes, unusual mouth treatment (embroidery rather than painting), wispy mohair wig, fully jointed. Appropriately redressed as a clown. $300.00. Circus accessories include a glass-eyed Shoenhut elephant.

Rare Steiff Doll: 14″, molded felt face, flesh color cotton body, all straw stuffed, blonde mohair hair, jointed at neck, shoulder and hip, sewn at shoulder. Breathtaking blue glass inset eyes. This beautiful doll has seamed arms and legs, stitched fingers, blush on cheeks and hands, painted eyebrows, lips and nostril openings. The original dress is one piece white cotton undersuit with lace trim at legs and top bodice, not easily removed, pink linen-type dress with blue leaf pattern, tiny pleats at side waist, pouf sleeves, two red snaps at back, white cotton socks, red felt shoes, red and navy felt hat with ribbon closure. This doll was purchased in Germany during the late 1930's. No evidence of an ear button. Paper tag is attached with thread to dress, "Lucie" has the bear face with watermelon mouth. Courtesy Nancy Catlin. $450.00 up.

Steiff "Lucki", 22″/55 cm., No. 88/755,1-3. Largest size of Dwarfs; pressed rubbed head, felt body, straw stuffed, fully jointed, painted black eyes, felt and cotton clothing. Circa 1957. Courtesy Pam and Amy Moorehead. $200.00.
Squirrel hand puppet, mohair, 1960. Courtesy Jason C. Moorehead, $25.00.
Moose shown in wild animal section.

"Mecki" and "Micki" Hedgehog Family (copyright *Diehl Film*): 6½"/17 cm. No. 88/717, pressed rubber heads, fully jointed felt bodies, bristle applied mohair, painted eyes, noses. Original clothing (Micki is missing white dotted kerchief). Made in 11"/28 cm. size: Micki carrying a spoon, Mecki a pipe; for display 20"/50 cm.. In 1936 Ferdinand Diehl made a full length animated film called *The Race Between the Hare and the Hedgehog* using bendable figures. In 1951 Diehl Films sold copyrights to the West German weekly magazine, *Hor Zu* for the immensely popular characters to be seen as a comic strip (1950's-early 1960's). Steiff concurrently bought the rights to make the toys which continues today. The deterioration factor (craquelure) of the early polyvinyl chloride makes investment in these a speculation. The formula has been perfected since. Courtesy Ruth L. Ruder. $45.00.

The Mecki Children, boy, "Macki"; girl, "Mucki": 5"/12 cm. No. 88/712 B and M, pressed rubber heads, fully jointed rubber bodies, mohair chest, black painted eyes and nose, bristly wig cap. Original clothes. He is from the 60's (glued on felt soles), she is from the 70's. Of greatest value as "props". $35.00 each in mint condition.

Panda, 2½", mohair, all straw, black bead eyes, brown floss nose, fully jointed. A desirable older German panda (possible Schuco). All courtesy Susan Roeder. $45.00 up.

X.
Steiff Animals Before 1940

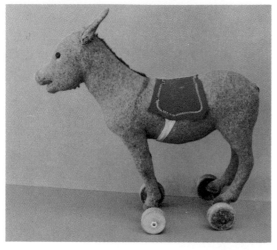

Steiff grey felt donkey, early 1900's: 14″ high, 16″ long, original shoe button eyes, open felt mouth, red felt saddle blanket (missing saddle). These wonderful early animals often seem to be missing tails. Note the fine posturing of donkey. Pewter button/ff underscored. Courtesy Rosella and Tony Santopietro. $400.00 up.

Steiff Bactrian Camel realistically depicted; 9″ long, rich brown felt and brown mohair mantle, all straw stuffed, steel wire supports, small shoe button eyes, leather harness, original red felt blanket. Rear wooden wheels replaced with Tinkertoys. Well rendered body contouring adds to the charm of this early pull toy. Camels are *rare*. Courtesy Rosella and Tony Santopietro. $350.00 up, if you can find one.

Steiff Dachshund, burnt orange felt, 8″ long, glass eyes, all straw, prong marks on left ear, brown floss nose, hand painted claws. Blue wooden eccentric (up/down) wheels. Before mohair became plentiful in the early 20th century, the Steiff line was made of felt. (Author). $175.00 up.

Pull toy, 12"/30 cm. high, gray mohair, air brushed toes, black shoe button eyes/white felt backing, white felt straw stuffed tusks sewn down, pull voice, wooden wheels on cast iron frame. Monkey is a Canadian souvenir, "Yes/No" type, not Schuco quality. Patent infringement. (Author). Elephant, $350.00; Monkey, $45.00.

Pug dog, 11" high, 14" long, chocolate brown and white mohair, straw stuffed, unjointed, black shoe button eyes, floss nose embroidered in the early Steiff animal style of contoured downward points, wide stitched mouth and claws, squeaker, cast iron spoked wheels. Rare 1910-15 Steiff pull toy. Courtesy Susan Passarelli. $275.00-300.00.

Steiff St. Bernard pull toy, 18" longer white mohair with inset spots, all straw, original glass eyes, pinkish-brown twisted yarn embroidered nose, mouth and claws (blends color-wise with markings), felt pads, bushy tail. Cast iron spoked wheels painted bronze. St. Bernard is one of the first pull toys that Steiff made. Production continued for a number of years. An heirloom. Circa 1907. Courtesy Diane Hoffman. $275.00 up.

Majestic: King "Leo", early pull toy, 12"/30 cm. high, 14"/38 cm. long nose to rump with a 9"/24 cm. tail. Yellow/white mohair, luxurious long pile mohair mane, all straw, rose floss nose, black floss mouth and claws, unjointed. Heavy steel frame enabling him to be ridden as well as pulled. This pristine example survived the delight of three sisters riding and pulling on cast iron spoked wheels. Early wheeled animals are much sought. Circa 1920. Courtesy Emogene Friant. $400.00.

Riding Zebra, 20" natural mohair striped, black glass eyes, felt pads, pull voice, steel frame, disc wheels with black rubber tires on cast iron frame. Animal has a wonderful face. Zebras, circus elephants and tigers are the most unusual and rare of the early riding animals. Ears should be replaced. Circa 1920. (Author). $300.00-400.00.

Riding Donkey, 21"/54 cm. high, 25"/69 cm. long, grey/white mohair, black glass eyes, felt hooves, grey/white mohair, steel frame, white rubber tires/blue disc wheels, red leather saddle (bridle missing), pull voice. Donkeys are the most common of riding animals. A 1950's example. (Author). $250.00-300.00.

"Tige", Buster Brown's dog, 9″ tall, mohair, straw stuffed, jointed head only, handblown *glass* eyes, embroidered nose and claws. Steiff often manufactured "characters" taken from storybooks and comic strips: Bugs Bunny and Mickey and Minnie Mouse. However, there is no proof positive that this happy faced dog was made by Steiff. Rare. Circa 1920. Courtesy Kay Bransky. $200.00 up.

"Bully" dog, 4″ high, mohair body and large ears, velvet face, straw stuffed, jointed head, amber glass eyes, floss nose and claws, "felt" collar around neck with round metal tag, "Bully." Orange (also on "Minnie Mouse") I.D. tag: "Steiff Original. 3214 Made in Germany." Bully was a German character dog featured in a children's story book written in German. Note there was a cat, Mini, also. Rare. Courtesy Kay Bransky. $250.00 up, with book.

Steiff "Bully", 3″, all velvet with inset markings, straw stuffed, unjointed, with the several undocumented characteristics: round white paper tag printed in black, "Bully, Steiff, Original" rimmed in *metal*; the neck ruff is sewn onto cotton tape. This variation from German storybook was made only a short time. Oversized (for the small dog) "rusty" ear button and original flattened brass bell. N.P.A.

231

Mickey Mouse, 7″ high, Steiff 1930's. All velvet, felt ears, soft stuffed, unjointed. Black oil cloth pie shaped eyes, painted mouth, original long thread whiskers. Cardboard innersoles. Black body, tan face, green pants/pearl button. Rare and desirable. $600.00 up.
Minnie Mouse, Steiff 5¼″ high, 1930's, all felt, straw stuffed, unjointed, oil cloth pie shaped eyes, painted mouth, original ear button, *orange* I.D. tag, cardboard innersoles, cotton skirt, stitched on undies, felt flower. Very rare. $500.00 up.
"Cockie", 5″/12 cm. No., 4276/12, standing, white/dark brown mohair, straw stuffed, jointed head, black and white glass eyes, black floss nose and mouth. Circa 1957. All courtesy Susan Passarelli. $45.00.

Expressive model: "Bully", 4½"/11 cm., later mohair with inset markings, velvet inset face, small glass eyes, floss nose, mouth handpainted, jointed head, remnant of *rectangular* link to hold missing bell. Right: same as above but all velvet, original brass bell on neck ribbon with stitched closure, pewter ear button/ff underscored. (Author). $85.00 each.

Cottontail, 10"/25 cm. long, black/white mohair, inset markings, all straw, black shoe button eyes/red felt backing, pink floss nose/mouth, sewn on white felt feet straw stuffed, early ear button. The cottontail was also made on eccentric (up/down) wheels during this 1910 period. (Author). $125.00 up.

Colt, standing, 11"/28 cm., pre-W.W. II example, printed ear button/ff underscored, sheared cotton gold plush, white blaze face, mohair mane and tail, all straw, brown glass eyes, white felt lined ears and orange hoofs. Steel framework in long legs. This model was available in 1957 in all mohair. (Author). $125.00.

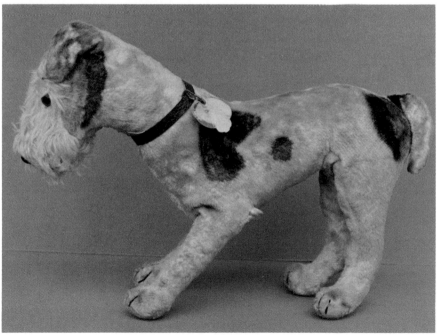

Fox Terrier, 10" high, 13" long, sheared rayon plush (velour), painted markings, straw stuffed, brown glass eyes, floss nose, mouth and claws (note these early animals had embroidered claws), ears tacked down, skinny legs, leather collar, pewter ear button/ff underscored, paper tag attached to collar. (Author). $150.00 up.

Polar Bears, 15″, white silky mohair, all straw stuffed, black glass bead eyes, black embroidered nose and claws, rigid neck, jointed legs to facilitate posing, white felt pads, tiny
Steiff ear button/ff underscored. Polar bears are solitary animals. These are sculpturesque
with the long neck and small head of the polar bear. A welcome addition to a Steiff collection. Rare. Courtesy Marian Swartz. $500.00 for pair.

"Susi", 7"/18 cm., cotton plush, all straw stuffed, jointed at neck, original red rayon bow showing the woven edge. Steiff used *only* ribbon with woven edges, but not all woven edged ribbon is from Steiff toys. Grisley and others used it. This rare cat has green glass eyes, pink floss nose and mouth, red floss claws. Paper chest tag with blue bear and watermelon (smiling) mouth, early ear button. Circa 1930's when cotton plush became popular. This covering matted and attracted soil. Hard to find in this mint condition. $95.00 up.

"Fluffy", cat, sitting, 4½"/11 cm., long pile mohair, straw stuffed, jointed head, green glass eyes, floss nose and mouth. Tail straight out. Early button. Circa 1930. Courtesy Susan Roeder. $65.00 up.

Steiff dog, early "Molly" type, 5"/12 cm., long pile, white/brown mohair, all straw, jointed head, brown glass eyes, black embroidered nose, mouth and claws on long feet. Long feet found on 1920's animals. Pewter button/ff underscored. $65.00.
Kitty, 4½"/11 cm., desirable long pile mohair, unjointed, green glass eyes, pink embroidered nose and mouth. Tail curled. They make a most personable pair. $65.00

Dog, 8″ high, 12″ long, shades of silver and brown long pile mohair, straw stuffed, shank-type brown glass eyes rimmed in black (unusual). Steiff occasionally used this "rimming" to add dimension. Black embroidered nose and claws, pink felt ears, pewter ear button/ff underscored, unjointed. Circa late 1930's, 1940's. Courtesy Nancy Roeder. $95.00 because of size and appeal.

"Chow-Chow Brownie", No. 21 is handwritten at factory on chest tag (bear with watermelon mouth); 6½″/17 cm. high, 7″/18 cm. long, long and short pile honey mohair, all straw with steel frame, brown glass eyes, black silk floss nose, mouth and claws, brown leather collar with brass studs. Pewter ear button/ff underscored. Circa 1930. (Author). $95.00 up.

XI.
Steiff Animals, 1940-Present

Margarete Steiff GmbH, Feature Catalogue E 1957/58.

Steiff Ark: tip-to-tip across top, 34″/86 cm.; width across center, 12″/31 cm.; overall height ark and house, 18″/36 cm. Trees and house are removable. House inside is stamped, "Made in Germany". In the late 1950's the Steiff factory distributed the ark as a store display for the retail trade. Included in a series of table top models were: saloon, barn, zoo, circus ring with animal train, puppet theater and ship. These are sought after today by collectors of the miniature animals. Courtesy Martha Gragg. $500.00 up.

Musical cat, 9½" high, tagged "Made in U.S. Zone Germany" (1945-52). Grey/white tabby markings, mohair, straw stuffed, jointed head only, green glass eyes, pink floss nose and mouth and claws. Unusual: music box in bottom, activated by pushing down on cat. Dressed in original red calico dress/3 Steiff buttons on back. Rare. Courtesy Susan Passarelli. $225.00-275.00.

Sitting Siamese 9"/25 cm. high, silky white mohair/shades of brown, all straw, prominent blue eyes, pink floss nose, open pink felt mouth and ear linings, red floss claws, jointed neck. Tag right front leg seam, "Made in U.S. Zone Germany". Circa 1950. A seldom-seen Siamese. (Author). $125.00.

"Mopsy" dog, 8½"/22 cm. No.4010/22. Also came in 5"/12 cm. size. Mohair, straw stuffed, jointed head, black and white glass eyes. One of more than 25 breeds of dogs made by Steiff. Circa 1969. $75.00.
"Lizzy" cat, 8½"/22 cm. No. 2713/22. Also made in 6"/15 cm. size, white mohair with grey tabby markings, all straw, green glass eyes, rose floss nose, mouth and claws. Tail *straight up* for "Lizzy". Courtesy Kay Bransky. $75.00.

"Susi" sitting, 4"/10 cm., No. 44G/3310, mohair, straw stuffed, green glass eyes, jointed head, nylon whiskers, brass bell attached to paper chest tag, ear button. "Susi" cats of whatever vintage are always sitting. Desirable. Courtesy Susan Roeder. $55.00.

Mama "Kitty Cat", 6½"/17 cm., No. 5317, fully jointed to stand and sit. This desirable model also came in 4"/10 cm. and 8½"/22 cm. size. $75.00.

Sharing her food with kittens: 4"/10 cm. "Tabby Cat" No. 1310,0 and 3"/07 cm., unjointed. These available in 5½"/14 cm. size and 6½"/17 cm. Note: white band around middle is definitive of Steiff for these standard tabbys. Popular prop to put in a doll's hand. Circa 1957-on. Courtesy Marge Meisinger. Photo by David Miller. Small: $45.00 up.

One can have eye-catching displays of kittens. Both are "Kitty Cat" with tabby markings, grey/white striped mohair, straw stuffed, green glass eyes. Large: 6½"/17 cm.; small, 4"/10 cm., fully jointed adds value. Courtesy Marge Meisinger. Large: $75.00. Baby: $55.00.

More rare "Topsy" cat, brown tabby markings, 3½"/8 cm. high, 5"/12 cm. long, short pile mohair, all straw, green glass eyes, original woven edge rayon bow to match rose stitched nose, ears backed with velvet, nylon whiskers. Brass bell. Circa 1964. $55.00.

"Snurry", 5"/12 cm. high, mohair, brown tabby markings, curled position with tail sewn to body, embroidered slits for sleeping eyes, rose floss nose. Unjointed. Hard to find. Circa 1964. Courtesy Susan Roeder. $65.00.

Large: chest tag "Tabby" 5½"/17 cm. No. 44/1314, grey/white striped mohair, all straw, green glass eyes, pink twine (not floss) nose, painted tongue and claws, nylon whiskers. This Tabby is never jointed. Brass bell attached to same linen thread as chest tag. Twill tape sewn into back seam right front leg, "Made in U.S. Zone Germany". Circa 1945-52. $65.00.
4" Tabby as above, No. 44/1310, $45.00.
Left: 3½"/07 cm. "Tabby" looks newborn. Courtesy Susan Roeder. $45.00 up.

Characteristic version of Puss 'N Boots: 17", black plush, straw stuffed, green glass eyes, open mouth with red felt tongue. Flashy original clothes: leather boots, red felt hat. Maker unknown. Courtesy Kay Bransky. $150.00-200.00.

Puss 'N Boots, 10″ mohair with tabby markings, all straw, long curved arms, jointed arms and head, green glass eyes, rose embroidered nose and mouth, no claws, nylon whiskers, white felt lined ears, red felt arm pads match felt boots with heavy cardboard soles. Detailed metal sword 4½″ long. Original red rayon ribbon that is not Steiff. Steiff Co. uses ribbon with woven edge. Rayon tag printed: "U.S. Zone Germany" tacked to right leg above boot. Steiff tags from this period are sewn into seam. Superior West Germany quality from 1945-52. Rare and desirable. Add value because a character adapted from a book. Courtesy Patricia R. Smith. $125.00 up.

White cat: 6½"/18 cm. white woolly plush, green eyes, red embroidered nose, pink felt lined ears with silver clip "RUF" in *right* ear, unjointed, straw stuffed, wire in tail. Unusual but not Steiff. Note cheaper construction. Steiff unequivocably used button only in *left ear* or other convenient spot such as a foot or fin, etc. $35.00.

Black cat, 7½"/20 cm., black long mohair, short white mohair snout, joined neck, wires in legs, early long feet, open felt mouth/pink airbrushed tongue, white felt lined ears, straw stuffed. Attributed to Steiff. Hard to find. Circa 1950's. Courtesy Susan Roeder. $75.00.

"Cosy Siam", 9" dralon, soft stuffed, rivet-type ear button, big blue eyes to match original blue ribbon, rose floss nose/mouth. 1970's. One might focus a collection on all of the cat-types made by Steiff. Discontinued. Replaced by "Cattie", a sitting Siamese cat 10" high. Courtesy Bev Murray. $65.00.

Awkward puppy: "Molly", 4"/10 cm., No. 68/3310, sitting, jointed head, long pile brown and white mohair, glass eyes, embroidered nose and mouth, long feet, Steiff button in ear. This is one of the few examples of Steiff depicting a mongrel. The "patina" of this toy does not lower value. Courtesy Marian Swartz. $55.00.

Fox Terrier "Foxy" sitting 6"/15 cm. high, white, black/brown mohair, all straw, brown glass eyes, black floss nose, mouth and claws, long feet, no pads. Tag: "U.S. Zone Germany" sewn in seam. 1945-52. Courtesy Bev Murray. $75.00.

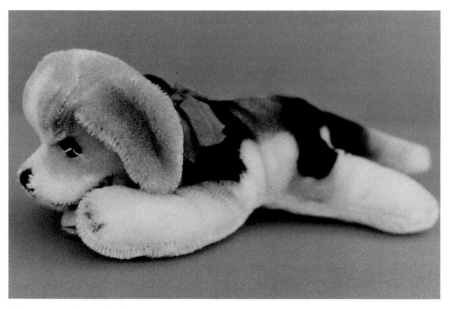

"Floppy Beagle", old chest tag/blue bear, 6½"/17 cm. long, white short pile mohair with shades of gold and black, hard stuffed head, soft body, black felt eyes/white stitch, open felt mouth with painted teeth, black floss nose and painted claws. A rare member of the Floppy Sleeping Animal series. Circa 1960's. (Author). $75.00.

"Tessie" Schnauzer, 11"/28 cm. high, 14"/35 cm. long, standing, light grey mohair, straw stuffed, jointed neck, lifelike oval shaped glass eyes, white iris, floss nose, mouth and claws, white shaggy mohair face, voice box. Circa 1950's on. Courtesy Susan Passarelli. $125.00 up.

Rare Dalmatian, 5½"/14 cm. begging (unusual), black glass eyes, floss nose and mouth, ears sewn down, sewn on jewelled crown, red taffeta white lined cape, jointed head, unusual closed mouth. A special issue for F.A.O. Schwarz (red plastic tag). Paper chest tag, "Original Steiff". Circa 1950-60. (Author). $195.00 up.

Copies of pets: "Bully", 4"/10 cm. long No. 11/1310, mohair, velvet snout, closed painted mouth, glass eyes, red leather collar. Spaniel "Cockie", 4"/10 cm., No. 29/2210, mohair (51% wool, 49% cotton), straw stuffed, jointed neck, brown glass eyes, velvet snout, ear button. "Dalmatian", 4"/10 cm. No. 15/3310, mohair, straw stuffed, brown glass eyes, black floss nose, velvet mouth with airbrushed tongue, jointed neck, red collar, ear button. All circa 1957-on. Courtesy Susan Roeder. $45.00 each.

Poodle "Snobby", 5½"/14 cm. No. 58/5314, long and short grey mohair, (also came in black or white), straw stuffed, brown glass dog's eyes include white glass "dot", glass bead nose, red felt tongue, velvet sewn-down ears, felt tail, jointed legs only. Red leather collar/rivet closure, rectangular link to attach paper tag. This toy combines the three Steiff materials of the era: mohair, velvet and felt. Common. Courtesy Susan Roeder. $45.00.

The ever-popular "Zotty", 11"/28 cm. No. 6328,1, $140.00.
Cocker Spaniel "Cockie", 8½"/35 cm. high, No. 29/2335,1, lying, black and white mohair, very soft, open felt mouth. Circa 1957-on. Courtesy Beth Everhart. Cost $15.00 in 1964. Now, $95.00 up.

"Floppy Cat", 11"/28 cm., also made in 6½"/18 cm. size. Sleepy, soft and cuddly, mohair/airbrushed markings and claws, hand embroidered eye lashes, pink twisted floss nose, nylon whiskers. No. 44/7328 in 1957, in 1977 change in numbering system. "Floppy Cockie" 11"/28 cm., No. 29/7328, also made in 6½"/18 cm. size. Long mohair with brown spots, black floss nose, black felt eyes with white floss stitch. Cute expression. Circa 1957-on. Courtesy Susan Roeder. $45.00 each.

Ginny walking her puppy with his own plaid blanket, missing leash. Steiff, 3¼″ high, No. 1308,0. The fox terrier "Foxy" was also made in 4, 6½, 8½, 11 and 13½″ sizes. Only the smallest is "Ginny's Pup". 1955-60. Ginny, (Author); Pup, courtesy Susan Roeder. $125.00.

Pekinese dog "Peky", 4″/10 cm., 6″/14 cm. high, No. 17a/1310, 1314, long honey color mohair, short mohair face with elaborate airbrushing, straw stuffed, brown glass eyes, floss nose. These are flashy but common. Circa 1950's-on. Courtesy Susan Roeder. $35.00, $50.00.

"Hexie", short hair Dachshund, 7"/20 cm. long, No. 18/1320, brown/yellow mohair, all straw, googly glass eyes, jointed head and ear button. Circa 1957-on. Common. $40.00.

Monkey, 13"/33 cm., light gold long pile mohair, tagged "Merry Thoughts Design No. 830/449", velvet face, ears, hands and feet, blue painted eyes. Soft stuffed head, straw torso and limbs. Courtesy Betty Shelley. $65.00.

"Waldi", 14"/35 cm. high sitting, No. 4140/35, long haired life size Dachshund, crylor fur, straw and soft stuffed, brown glass eyes, cryor pads, unusual "barking" squeaker, jointed head. 1971-1977. (Author). $150.00.

Hopping Rabbit, 5½"/14 cm. high, 10"/25 cm. long, No. 36/1314, white and brown mohair, all straw, brown glass eyes, floss nose and mouth, felt lined ears. This is the middle size. Early 1950 version with softer colors. Missing bell. Body contouring is a great favorite among collectors. (Author). $65.00 up.

"Record Hansi" on coaster, pumps when pulled along, 10"/25 cm. No. 36/325, honey mohair, all straw, fully jointed, open felt mouth with felt teeth, pink embroidered nose, automatic voice, red wooden wheels. Steiff has made these animals on "up/down" wheels since 1910. Bears, rabbits and monkeys were favorites. Delightful 1950's toy. Rabbits are one of the most popular collectibles. Courtesy Rosella and Tony Santopietro. $150.00.

"Niki", 11"/28 cm. No. 36/5328,2, beige/grey mohair, all straw, glass eyes, jointed to be very poseable, open felt mouth, usually the ears are erect. The smallest (5½"/14 cm. and 6½"/17 cm.) do not have open mouths. "Niki" is favored by collectors because of his long feet on jointed legs. Courtesy Kay Bransky. $150.00 up.

Rabbits: Lying, 4½"/11 cm. long, 2½"/06 cm. high, No. 36/2306, brown/white mohair, straw, jointed neck, black/white glass eyes, pink twisted floss nose, nylon whiskers, velvet lined ears, original red rayon woven edged bow. Chest tag, "Original Steiff" as seen on the 1960's animals. Sitting: 4½"/11 cm., mohair, straw stuffed, jointed head, red embroidered nose/mouth, brown glass eyes, felt lined ears, nylon whiskers, prong ear button. Running: 4½"/11 cm. long, 3¼"/08 cm. high, No. 36/1308, mohair, straw, unjointed, brown glass eyes, red floss mouth and nose, nylon whiskers, felt lined ears. Courtesy Susan Roeder. $45.00 up each.

"Manni" Rabbit, begging, 8"/20 cm. No. 3020/20, white mohair with shades of brown and grey, all straw stuffed, jointed head, glass eyes, open felt mouth. In 1968 "Manni" was made in five sizes from 4"/10 cm. to 22"/55 cm. Older version. Courtesy Kay Bransky. $125.00.

Top: "Begging Rabbit", 11"/28 cm. high, No. 4328,2; brown/white mohair, jointed head, closed mouth, tag, "Made in U.S. Zone, Germany", (1945-52), straw stuffed, glass eyes, pink floss nose/mouth, squeaker, long floppy ears. $125.00-150.00.
Right: 11½"/30 cm. (large) puppet, white/brown mohair, straw stuffed head, glass eyes, red floss nose/mouth. 1960's example. $70.00.
Bottom: Lying Rabbit and Hopping Rabbit (found elsewhere). Courtesy Susan Passarelli.

Lamb "Lamby", 8½"/20 cm. high, No. 46/65220, white wool plush that mats easily, all straw, green glass eyes, red floss nose/mouth, felt lined ears. Also came in 4"/10 cm., 5½"/14 cm., 11"/28 cm. and largest was 13½"/35 cm. Early 1950's. $75.00.

Rare black lamb, 4"/10 cm. high, not catalogued but pictured 1957 only. Note white spot on top of head. $85.00 up.

"Grissy" Donkey, 10"/27 cm. high, No. 3605/27 (1978), grey dralon plush, soft stuffed, black plastic eyes, airbrushed nose and mouth. Farm animals have been made by Steiff since production began. The new and the old blend well. (Author). C.S.P.

"Cow", 6½"/17cm. high, 9"/24 cm. long, No. 3910/17, mohair with Hereford markings, black/white glass googly eyes, airbrushed nostrils, open felt mouth, velvet at wide chest, well formed felt udders. Also a 5"/12 cm. size. A "Cosy Calf" was in the 1968 line. Missing collar and bell. The mohair cow is hard to find. $65.00.

"Floppy Lamb", 7"/17 cm. long, No. 5620/17, wooly mohair, soft stuffed, stitched sleeping eyes. Unusual rayon I.D. tag on left ear. (Author). $45.00

Farmyard Animals. Left: Donkey 8½"/22 cm., grey/white mohair, straw stuffed, unjointed, glass eyes, painted mohair nose, stiff black mohair mane. Wonderful face on this large early example. $150.00-175.00.

Platform pull toy Cow, 9½" high, 14" long, hide covered paper mache body, bone horns, move head from side to side to "moo". German, 1890's. $295.00.

"Lamby", 5½"/14 cm. No. 46/6514. $55.00.

Pink felt pig, 2¾"/07 cm. high, 4"/10 cm. long, straw stuffed, unjointed, blue glass eyes, floss nose/mouth. 1970's. All courtesy Susan Passarelli. $40.00.

253

"Lamby", 4"/10 cm. woolly plush. "Bayer" is the brand name for synthetic dralon plush found on reverse side of this chest tag. Green eyes, pink floss nose/mouth, original blue ribbon with bell, air-brushed hooves. Purchased in West Germany early 1950's. $45.00.

"Danny" 13" high, black rayon plush, rayon mask molded face, felt hooves, tagged "Gund Manufacturing". Delightful and rare character taken from Walt Disney Productions movie, "So Dear To My Heart". 1947. N.P.,A.

"Floppy Lamby", 13"/35 cm. nose to rump, "Bayer" plush, soft stuffed, brown embroidered sleep eyes, rattle in right foot (unusual) marketed as baby's toy. Tag in right shoulder seam, "U.S. Zone, Germany". Purchased there in early 1950's. Note the unusually large size. All courtesy Carolyn Altfather. $135.00.

"Baby Goat', standing 9"/22 cm. high No. F4/6322,0, white and light brown mohair, all straw, green eyes, felt horns, ears and tail back, black floss nose and mouth. Note body patterning similar to "Lamby". This animal was also made on eccentric (up/down) wheels. Circa 1950. Courtesy Bev Murray. $75.00.

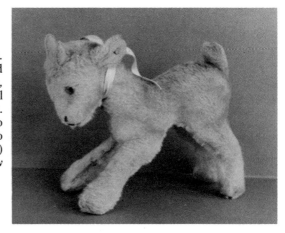

"Guinea Pig", 5"/12 cm., 1965, dralon and cotton, soft stuffed, black embroidered nose and mouth, plastic black and white eyes, white felt feet. $25.00.

"Porcupine", 4"/10 cm., 1965, dralon and cotton, straw stuffed, painted face, felt ears and feet, black bead eyes, corduroy stomach. Button on left foot, No. 2310,00. Courtesy Craig Roeder. $35.00.

Goldfish, 26"/50 cm. No. 2350,01, yellow/orange mohair (also available in blue), straw and cotton stuffed, glass eyes with mohair backing, stuffed felt open mouth, Steiff button on dorsal fin. Both colors came in 5"/10 cm. and 11"/22 cm. sizes. Long production: 1965-78 when the large size was discontinued. Felix the Cat, vinyl head, jointed wood body. $45.00. (Author). Fish, $150.00 up.

"Pony", standing, 5"/12 cm. No. 56/1312, mohair, unjoined, all straw, brown glass eyes, painted mouth, red floss bridle/yellow felt discs, red leather saddle, felt ears with prong button. Synthetic bristle mane and tail. $55.00.

"Chimpanzee", 4"/10cm. No. 090/5310, brown mohair, black bead eyes, felt face, ears, hands and feet (mitten type, no stitching), fully jointed. 1960 exactly. White, 5"/12 cm. No. 9/5315. Add $10.00 because of rare white color. Chimpanzees made in ratio, 2 white to 7 brown. Courtesy Susan and Craig Roeder. $35.00, $45.00 up.

Pig, 3"/07 cm. high, 6"/15 cm. long, No. 64/1407, pink short pile mohair, blue glass eyes, pink felt mouth, snout and ears (prong marks), curled sisal tail, original red twisted cord sewn on, unjointed. Germany has much pig lore, especially at Christmas. Courtesy Susan Roeder. $55.00, this size.

The most illusive of the Steiff collectibles: "Eric the Bat," 8"/21 cm. tall, mohair, straw stuffed, glass bead eyes and nose, jointed arms and legs. Mohair covered wire forelimbs modified to form wings. The same idea of wire appendages was used on the lobster and spider. Collectors feel that this 1960's animal is "cute", as well as extremely rare. Courtesy Kay Bransky. $250.00 up.

Lion Cub, lying, 11"/28 cm. that is not a Steiff but has similar characteristics: yellow and white woolly plush, soft and cuddly, green *glass* eyes, rust color yarn (not floss) embroidered nose with black stitched outline and mouth, black stippled snout and airbrushed pads (same as Steiff). Thin nylon whiskers, (not fishing line-type used by Steiff). Yellow rayon tag sewn into right ear seam, "Designed by Character, Made in U.S.A." Courtesy Vera Tiger. $15.00.

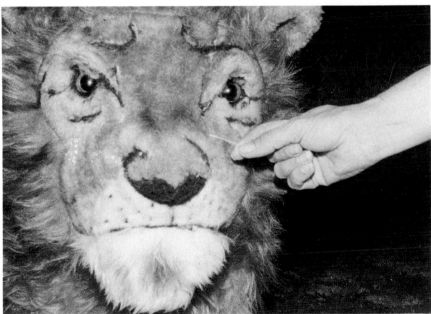

Example of non-Steiff Lion: 40"/102 cm. long, 27"/68 cm. high, synthetic plush, haunches and back have steel framework for contouring, stuffed with styrofoam pellets that can simulate straw, yellow glass eyes, sewn on ears, airbrushed facial markings, nose and claws (not embroidered). Note the absence of airbrushed pads that Steiff Lions have and a less luxurious mane and tail. There is a linen thread on face that could be mistaken for that from a Steiff paper tag. Since 1982 Steiff has designed some of their large Studio Decor animals in a crouching position, for example, the Puma. Made by Toy Animals, Inc., S.C. Courtesy Sharon Griffiths, C.S.P.

257

Very rare Steiff spider, "Spidy", 2½"/06 cm. high, 4¾"/12 cm. long, chest tag, no button. White mohair with pink, green and brown markings, straw stuffed, unjointed, *three* black bead eyes, 8 mohair covered wire legs. Not a popular shelf item and very few were made. Circa 1960's. Courtesy Susan Passarelli. $200.00 up.

"Crabby", 11"/28 cm. long, 9"/23 cm. wide, black glass eyes, mouth is two strands of red cord tied in center, 8 mohair covered wire legs, button under tail, left side, No. 338/2328,00. The same year (1964) a smaller lobster was made of felt. Both relate to the zodiac sign. Rare. $175.00.

"Gaty", 28"/70 cm. long, No. 0970,30, green, black and brown decorated mohair, green eyes rimmed in black, bulging eye sockets, red felt mouth, teeth outlined in white felt, four brown felt claws, green felt spinal ridge with button. The dinasour and alligator are considered the most unusual of the Steiff animals. (Author). $150.00.

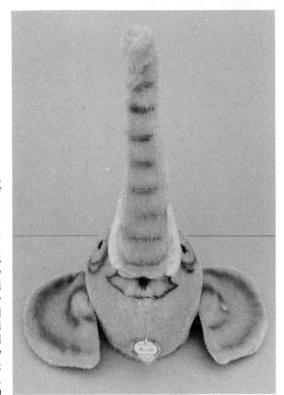

Undocumented Elephant Head is a showpiece as well as a trophy of the collector's successful stalk; 6½"/17 cm. high, 12"/30 cm. long, no yellow I.D. tag on ear, prong type button, old chest tag. In the late 1960's-early 1970's Steiff produced a series of "trophy heads" including the Rhino and Lion. None have I.D. tags. They seem not to be given a serial number. These are unique and easily recognizable by the wood backing with two holes. Short grey mohair/airbrush markings, black glass eyes, felt tusks sewn down, pink felt nose. (Author). $300.00 up.

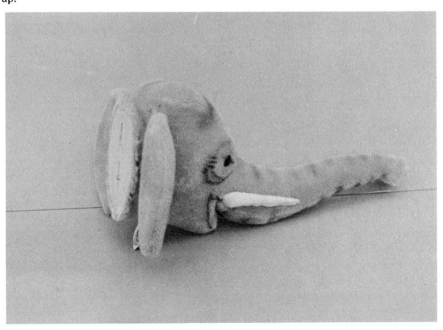

"Kangoo", 20"/50 cm. No. 43/4350, begging, white mohair with shades of brown and grey, brown glass soulful eyes, embroidered black floss nose with lifelike downward *contoured* points, also characteristic of some early Teddy Bears; floss claws, jointed arms and neck, felt lined ears. Velvet Joey, 3½"/09 cm., in pouch with glass eyes, floss nose and mouth, felt ears. All Courtesy Carolyn Altfather. $250.00 up.

Largest Moose, "Moosy", 10"/25 cm. high, No. 604/13. A 5½"/14 cm. also available. Limited production. Shades of brown mohair, black glass eyes, ruled felt antlers, all straw. Purchased at F.A.O. Schwarz for $9.50. Circa 1964. Rare. Courtesy Margaret Moorehead. $175.00 up.

"Wild Boar", 8"/20 cm. high, 11"/28 cm. long, No. 640/1320,08. Fearsome mohair with prickly coat, all straw, intense blue glass eyes, jointed head. Also available in 4"/10 cm. size. The large one is more unusual. There is most investment potential in the *large* Steiff animals. This toy sold for $9.50 in 1964. Courtesy Kay Bransky. $175.00 up.

"Bison", 11"/28 cm. high, 15"/38 cm. long, unjointed, short mohair in shades of brown, long pile mohair hump, tail and head, ruled felt horns, brown glass eyes, appealing detail and a bit of "Americana". Circa 1960's. Courtesy Susan Roeder. $175.00.

Dromedary, 13"/35 cm. No. 42/1535,0, largest size camel made. Light brown wool plush, velvet face and legs, glass eyes, felt ears, painted nose, straw stuffed, unjointed. Note: the leg-hoof construction is similar to the llama. Circa 1957. Rare. Courtesy Susan Passarelli. $225.00.

Llamas: 17"/43 cm. high, No. 425/1343, long mohair body, shaved *mohair* face and legs with bifurcated hoof, brown glass eyes, straw stuffed, unjointed. Collectors are stalking the older and unusual large Steiff animals. Small: 11"/28 cm. (also available in 6½"/17 cm. size). Large: 1964-68 only. Courtesy Susan Roeder. $225.00, $85.00.

Llama: 6½"/17 cm. high, No. 425/1317, white mohair, white velvet face and legs, straw stuffed, unjointed, velvet ears, prong ear button, old chest tag. Velvet replaces shaved mohair in smallest size. Circa 1964. Hard to replace. Courtesy Susan Roeder. $65.00.

Tiger: 13½"/35 cm., reclining, vivid oranges and black, 51% wool, 49% cotton (mohair), paper chest tag attached with plastic, green glass eyes rimmed in black, nylon whiskers, pink embroidered nose, airbrushed and embroidered claws, very life-like. Circa 1972. Courtesy Susan Roeder. $95.00.

"Caught in the Act". Fox, begging posture, lifesize 25"/64 cm., natural color mohair, straw stuffed, jointed head, glass eyes, black embroidered nose, black tipped ears and paws, open felt mouth with long felt tongue, missing two fang teeth; produced 1950's-1960's. Steiff mohair rabbit. Fox is *rare*. Courtesy Kay Bransky. $450.00 up.

Left: 16"/40 cm. high, 28"/71 cm. long, No. 0910/60, vivid mohair striping, straw head, straw and cotton body, green eyes, pink floss nose outlined in black, three floss claws, airbrushed pads, nylon whiskers, prong ear button. $350.00-400.00.

Second from left: 22"/56 cm. Steiff counterfeit, complete with implanted prong ear button, tigered mohair, hard stuffed cotton (no straw); note stubby snout, yarn (not floss) nose without black outline, no stitched mouth or claws, yellow glass eyes/round pupil, same stippled snout and airbrushed pads, wrong posturing (this Steiff model lies high on shoulders), facial markings not consistent with Steiff. America, circa 1950's. $95.00-125.00.

Sitting: 25"/64 cm. white/yellow and black markings (faded). Airbrushed colors fade and must be protected from light. Green glass eyes, pink floss nose, open pink felt mouth with four wooden teeth, three stitched claws, mohair pads/cardboard innersoles. Shiny Steiff ear button. $350.00 up.

Right: 29"/74 cm., same as far left. (Author). $350.00-400.00, or $13.00 per inch of length, without tail. Steiff made large mohair lying tigers, 1957-77.

Tigers. Left, tagged, "Japan", 7"/18 cm. long, sparse stripes on mohair, ears sliced into straw head. Note the identical body contouring. Center: 6½"/17 cm. high, 9"/25 cm. long, No. 70/1317,0, standing, yellow black tigered mohair, green glass eyes, pink twisted floss nose, nylon whiskers. Right: 5½"/14 cm. high, 6"/15 cm. long. Same as above. Circa 1960's. Courtesy Christl Kober. Japan, $15.00; Steiff, $55.00, $45.00.

"Tiger Cub", 4"/10 cm. high No. 70/3310, sitting, natural shaded mohair, straw stuffed, jointed neck, green glass eyes, painted and embroidered nose, *curled* tail. Circa 1957. Center: older "Tiger Cub", 4"/10 cm. jointed neck, tail is straight out, coloring of mohair is richer. Steiff used captivating names for animals such as "Nosy". Rhinoceros, 4"/10 cm. No. 55/1310, standing grey short mohair, grey felt horn and ears, painted and embroidered mouth, glass googly eyes, braided floss tail, straw stuffed. These animals desirable for the Steiff miniature "Zoo". Courtesy Susan Roeder. $45.00 each.

265

King Lion "Leo", 12"/30 cm. high, 20"/50 cm. long, No. 48/2350, lying, natural color mohair, straw and soft stuffed, orange glass eyes (as opposed to the usual green eyed tigers), rose floss nose, black floss mouth and claws. $275.00 up.

"Lion Cub", 6"/15 cm. high, No. 48/5316, fully jointed, yellow-brown mohair, squeaker. Part of the "Lion Family" that includes Mama and Papa. Circa 1957-on. $65.00.

Giraffe, 31"/75 cm. high, No. 0750/75, yellow mohair spotted orange, black glass eyes, mohair pads, steel structure, *open* felt mouth, Circa 1968. The 1950's giraffe had closed mouth. The later version is more attractive. Another case where oldest is not always best. (Author). $225.00.

King Lion "Leo", lying, 45"/112 cm., the largest size made during the 1950-60 period. Yellow/white mohair, long curly mane, soft and cuddly. A decorator piece in this life size. Courtesy Vera Tiger. $550.00 up.

Shown with 16"/60 cm. "Lion Cub", lying, yellow/brown spotted mohair. Courtesy Vera Tiger. $200.00 up.

Lion "Cub", 19"/48 cm. long, lying, soft and cuddly, yellow-brown spotted mohair, long pile mohair lining ears and chin, green glass eyes, rose floss nose, black floss mouth and claws. 1957-on. $275.00 up.
Lounging Leopard, 20"/50 cm. long, No. 5320/50, dralon fur, super soft, yellow glass eyes, rose floss nose, black floss mouth, prong ear button. Circa 1972-75. Courtesy Susan Bowles. $95.00 up.

"Lion Cub", 5½"/14 cm. long, standing, yellow and brown mohair, all straw, yellow/green eyes, pink floss nose, black stitched mouth, nylon whiskers, unjointed. 1957-on. Courtesy Nancy Nelson. $55.00.

Lion sitting, 5"/12 cm. high, yellow-brown mohair with long mane, unjointed. King Lion "Leo", standing, 11"/28 cm. long. These toys have withstood many hours of play and remain in mint condition with chest tags. 1960's. Courtesy Christl Kober. 5", $45.00; 11", $65.00; 4½" standing, $45.00.

"Lea", 4½"/11 cm. No. 48/3311, sitting, yellow-brown mohair, unjointed, rose twisted floss nose, orange glass eyes, airbrushed markings and claws, well contoured haunches, chest tag, "Lea". Sweet miniature lioness. Hard to find., 1957-69. $55.00 up.

Compare to tagged "Ideal Toy Corp." Lion, made in Japan, with less detailed markings, woolly plush, sliced in ears, pale pink thread (not twisted floss) nose, shorter tail. Both lions straw stuffed. Courtesy Susan Roeder. $15.00.

Elephant, 3"/07 cm. high, the smallest made, all short grey mohair, straw stuffed, black bead eyes with red airbrushed shading, white plastic tusks, grey felt ears/prong type button. Prong type buttons were easily dislodged from felt ears. Felt circles for pads, nails airbrushed, braided floss tail. Rare red felt blanket with Steiff insignia enhances value. Hans Otto Steiff identified this as the special animal for the 75th Anniversary in 1955. Courtesy Susan Roeder. $95.00 up.

Elephants. Left: 8½"/22 cm. high, No. 20/6322,01, standing, beige-grey mohair, straw stuffed, unjointed, googly glass eyes (these black/white glass eyes also seen on Japan made animals), felt nose, mouth and tusks, grey felt pads, airbrushed toes, missing circus blanket. Also available in 3"/07 cm., 4"/10 cm., 6½"/17 cm. and 13½"/35 cm. sizes. Circa 1957. $100.00-125.00.
Right: "Cosy Trampy", 8"/20 cm. high, No. 20/6620, blue-grey with pink dralon plush (Bayer), filled with foam rubber, unjointed, googly glass eyes, plastic pads, felt open mouth, original bell on red plastic collar. Of great appeal to children and collectors. Different. A new item in 1950's-on. Courtesy Susan Passarelli. $75.00.

"Okapi", 17"/43 cm., No. 324/6343, mohair (*rare* in this animal). In 1964 an 11"/28 cm. and 5½"/14 cm. were available in velvet which continued. The tactile quality of the mohair is far superior. This impressive large size sold for $12.00 in 1964. Courtesy Kay Bransky. $225.00 up.

"Okapi", 6½"/14 cm. high, highly stylized airbrushed velvet, straw stuffed, glass eyes, painted nose and mouth, synthetic horsehair-type mane, braided floss tail, felt ears, prong marks, unjointed. 1964-on. $55.00.

"Zebra", 8½"/22 cm. high, No. 1420/22 on I.D. tag, rivet type button, short mohair, wonderfully striped, straw stuffed, small brown glass eyes, painted nose, unjointed. Desirable animal. 1957-on. Courtesy Susan Roeder. $75.00 this size.

Panther, 20″/50 cm. No. 5322/35, pure black dralon fur, super soft and supple, lounging with legs dangling. 1973-1980. Striking yellow glass eyes, rose floss nose with black painted highlights, nylon whiskers. A prime example featuring the reality of the stuffed animal kingdon. (Author). $150.00.

Baboon "Coco", 5½″/14 cm. high, No. 9a/1314, standing, short mohair shades of beige, pink felt face and ears with airbrushed detail, green eyes, beige felt feet with stitched toes and separate thumbs, jointed head only, red collar rivet closure. 1957-1968. Courtesy Susan Roeder. $45.00 in this largest size.

271

"Jocko", Chimpanzee, 13½"/35 cm., I.D. tag 0020/35, fully jointed brown mohair, straw stuffed, inset/stitching brown glass eyes, felt face (open/close mouth), ears and stitched hands, squeaker. Old chest tag, rivet type button in ear (present day button is on foot). Chimpanzees were one of the first Steiff stuffed animals. Available in 7 different sizes. Plentiful. (Author). $125.00 this size.

"Record Peter", 10"/25 cm. monkey on coaster, fully jointed, stitched fingers (hands and feet bent to circle bars), glass eyes, painted face, all straw. Circa 1957-1968. $135.00 up. "Elephant", 4"/10 cm. high, grey mohair, googly glass eyes, grey felt ears, red felt ruff, plastic tusks. Many of the older animals have plastic tusks. 1957-on. Courtesy Shirlee Glass. $45.00.

"Bambi", standing, 5½"/14 cm. high, light brown spotted velvet with mohair insets on chest and tail, black embroidered nose, black glass eyes with *plastic backing* ("big eyes") to differentiate between "Roe". Unjointed, prong type ear button. Copyright *Walt Disney Productions*, not exported to all countries. 1950's-on. Courtesy Susan Roeder. $35.00.

Paper Christmas plate purchased in West Germany in 1954, 10"/25 cm. diameter, 1½"/2.7 cm. deep. Note depiction of Steiff forest animals. The ear button is evident on the fawn. Courtesy Carolyn Altfather. $15.00.

"Bocky", buck deer, 9″/22 cm. high, No. 1811/22, yellow/brown short pile mohair, black glass eyes, black floss nose (white stitch as highlight), airbrushed hooves, double weight felt antlers. Circa 1973. $65.00.

"Perri", 5″/12 cm., No. 2040/12 (Copyright *Walt Disney Productions*), white/brown mohair, black glass eyes with white felt backing, cut out white felt feet. Main character in Disney nature film. Circa 1968. All Courtesy Carolyn Altfather. $45.00.

"Possy", squirrel, 4″/10 cm., No. 2005/10, short and long mohair, shades of grey (also made in brown), straw stuffed, black glass bead eyes, black floss nose and mouth, unjointed (double thread tied around neck to suggest jointing separation), well contoured haunches, old chest tag, prong ear button. 1968-on. Courtesy Susan Roeder. $45.00.

274

Left: "Xorry", standing, 4½"/11 cm. long, No. 280/1311, natural mohair, straw stuffed, tiny brown glass eyes, unjointed, ear button. Cute face. 1964-on. Courtesy Susan Roeder. $55.00.
Right: "Snuffy", 7"/18 cm. high, No. 3515/18, 80% dralon, 20% cotton, soft stuffed, detailed airbrush shading, brown plastic eyes, black floss nose and mouth, black velvet backed ears to match black plush feet. Large rivet gold ear button, made in Austria. (Author). C.S.P. The old and the new look well together. Beautiful foxtails.

"Cosy Fuzzy", fox, 8½"/22 cm., No. 280/3622 in 1964 when it cost $7.00. In 1968 No. 4900/22. Dralon with inset orange markings, synthetic fiber filled, glass eyes, black velvet pads and ear backing, black floss nose with white highlight stitch, nylon whiskers. $65.00.
"Cosy Zicky", baby goat, 10"/25 cm. No. 4960/25 in 1968, dralon with inset black/white markings, synthetic fiber filled, green glass eyes, floss nose, felt horns and lined ears, blue ribbon with bell. The early "Cosy" line of animals have their own charm and are becoming hard to find. All Courtesy Carolyn Altfather. $65.00.

"Mountain Lamb", catalogued in 1964, No. 462/1312; in 1968 given new name, "Ram Snucki", and 6½"/18 cm. and 8½"/22 cm. sizes added; 5"/12 cm. high, No. 3500/12, mohair, all straw, ruled white felt horns, green glass eyes, rose floss nose. Hard to find. Courtesy Earl Meisinger. $55.00.

"Nagy", beavers, 10"/25 cm., 6½"/17 cm. and 4"/10 cm. all found in 1964. Long mohair pointed with white and short brown mohair, straw stuffed, black glass eyes, largest has interesting detailed felt hands backed with mohair, three fingers and a thumb. Two double weight felt teeth in open felt mouth, jointed heads. Note the substantial felt tails, ruled. Courtesy Susan Roeder. $175.00, $85.00, $45.00.

"Raccy", racoon, 4"/10 cm. high, No. 126/4310, long pile mohair, straw stuffed, life-like airbrushed face, brown glass eyes, dark brown floss nose, white felt cut-out feet, jointed at neck. Ear button with prongs. Circa 1964. Courtesy Susan Roeder. $45.00.

Porcupine (Hedgehog), 5"/12 cm., begging, No. 37/4312, silver tipped long mohair, straw stuffed, black bead eyes, black floss nose, pink felt ears, jointed head, prong marks. Available 1957-1970. This animal has an "antique look". Desirable prop. $55.00.
Porcupine (Hedgehog), "Joggi", stiffened mohair, straw stuffed, black bead eyes, pink felt ears, white cut-out feet, unjointed, prong button. In 1964 No. 370/2312. Hard to find. Courtesy Susan Roeder. $55.00.

"Murmy", groundhog, 4½"/10 cm., No. 505/2310, white/tan long pile mohair, all straw, black glass eyes, white cut-out feet. Note egg-shaped head. Limited production. Circa 1964. Courtesy Shirlee Glass. $55.00.

"Diggy", badger, 4"/10 cm. high, No. 185/4310, striking black, white and orange markings on mohair, all straw, pink floss nose and mouth, bright orange glass eyes, white felt cut-out paws, unjointed. Rare. Circa 1964. Shelf price, $2.50. (Author). $65.00.

278

Two main kinds of the many species of seals are the eared seals and earless, of which the common harbor seal is earless. Top: large spotted seal, 14"/35 cm. long, short beige mohair, all straw, large black glass eyes, rose floss nose, small pink felt ears. Circa 1950's. (Author). $95.00 up.

"Robby", dralon spotted seal, 12"/30 cm. long, soft stuffed, earless, white nylon whiskers. C.S.P.

"Oily", grey dralon, 6"/15 cm. long, soft stuffed, small plastic eyes, pink floss nose. Made in Austria. C.S.P.

"Wally", walrus, 6"/15 cm. long, dralon, all soft, blue eyes, pink floss nose, white felt tusks, large gold Steiff button riveted on left flipper. C.S.P. Courtesy Susan Roeder.

"Slo", turtle, 5½"/14 cm. No. 65/2314, short brown mohair, yellow underside, black bead eyes, embroidered mouth, felt claws, plastic shell sewn on. Available 1957-1977. Courtesy Susan Roeder. $35.00.

"Robby", begging seal, 4"/10 cm., No. 630/4310, short white mohair with grey and green spots, pink floss nose, black floss mouth, unjointed. Courtesy Susan Roeder. $45.00.
"Paddy", walrus, 5½"/14 cm. high, (also available in 4"/10 cm. and 8½"/22 cm. sizes), beige mohair with brown and green spots, black/white googly glass eyes, rose floss nose, stiffened long mohair moustache, nylon whiskers, plastic tusks. Shelf price in 1964, $4.00. Discontinued in 1968. Walrus is harder to find than seal. (Author). $65.00.

"Slo", 14"/35 cm., all mohair, beautiful markings, open felt mouth, black glass bead eyes, old tag. $19.50 in 1970. Courtesy Marge Vance. $95.00.
Velvet "Froggy", 4"/10 cm., sitting No. 2370/10, glass eyes rimmed with grey. Velvet "Froggy" is now shown dangling only. Courtesy Marge Vance. $35.00.

280

"Pieps", white mouse, 3½"/08 cm., white mohair, straw stuffed, pink glass bead eyes, black glass bead nose, white felt ears, tail and cut-out feet, nylon whiskers, unjointed. Available 1957-1974. Courtesy Susan Roeder. $25.00.

"Wittie", begging owl, 4"/10 cm., mohair in colors, straw stuffed, oversized black rimmed plastic eyes, black bristle topknot; felt beak, wings; wire in tail and feet, jointed neck. Made as large as 13½"/35 cm. This is the most common size. Courtesy Susan Roeder. $35.00.

Early Penguin, 8½″/22 cm. high, short white mohair, airbrushed to black, brown glass eyes, orange felt feet and bill, black velvet flippers. Penguins have been in Steiff production for many years. This is a replica of one of the 12 species, not the king penguin they made as "Peggy". 1950's only. Courtesy Susan Roeder. $75.00.

"Goose", standing, 5"/12 cm., No. 30/6312, open wings, white/grey mohair, straw stuffed, black glass bead eyes, orange felt beak and feet with rust felt sole. Also available in 6"/15 cm. size. 1957-on. Courtesy Earl Meisinger. $45.00 up.

Lying duck, 5"/14 cm. No. 22/2314, gloriously colored mohair, felt feet and bill. Available 1957-1978 when Steiff changed bird to washable plush. Courtesy Susan Bowles. $45.00.

Wool miniature "Cock", 3½"/08 cm., No. 34/1508, metal feet (plastic feet replaced metal in 1971), black/white googly glass eyes, felt beak and comb. Early yellow mohair duck, 1¾"/04 cm. felt and metal webbed feet, felt bill, extended wings. Wool miniature duck, 2"/05 cm., yellow (also avaiable in colors), glass bead eyes/felt backing, felt bill and metal feet. All 1957-on. Courtesy Bev Murray. $20.00.

Chickens, 2½"/06 cm. and 1½"/04 cm., No. 35/1506 and 1504. Bright yellow mothproof wool miniatures, metal feet, black glass bead eyes. 1957-on. Courtesy Earl Meisinger. $15.00-20.00.

"Teddyli", bear, 4"/12 cm. No. 12/712, mohair jointed head, straw stuffed, velvet face, brown glass eyes, rubber body, original clothes of felt overalls and skirt. "Bibbie", rabbit, 4"/12 cm., No., 36/312M, mohair head jointed at neck, straw stuffed, brown glass eyes, velvet ears, original clothes, rubber body. "Cocoli", chimp, 4"/12 cm., No. 91/9a/712, felt face framed in mohair, back of head is black velvet, green glass eyes, felt ears, all original/blue felt jacket, rubber body, painted-on black shoes with felt soles. The various costumed animals made by Steiff are much sought. They are always colorfully dressed. Rare. Courtesy Nancy Roeder. $95.00 up each.

Hide-A-Gift-Bunny, 6"/15 cm., No. 3174/15 and No. 3172/15. Head and arms are mohair, glass eyes, rose floss nose and mouth, jointed head, dressed in felt. Inside is hollow to hide small gifts. They can also be used as hand puppets; unlike most, these can stand without support. A German inspiration introduced in 1968. By 1970, Teddy, Fox, Tabby Cat and Cocker Spaniel were available. Courtesy Earl Meisinger. $45.00 up.

"Waldili", dachshund as hunter, 9½"/26 cm., No. 770/26; mohair head, hands and feet, straw stuffed head jointed at neck, sewn on felt arms, soft stuffed, rigid torso/legs hard stuffed cotton, brown glass eyes, embroidered black nose, airbrushed claws, felt pads with cardboard innersoles, original green felt hunting suit, wooden rifle painted brown, 6¼" long, prong type button. One of the most charming and sought after Steiff toys of the past 50 years. Circa 1971. Courtesy Diane Hoffman. $250.00 up.

"Zipper Nauty", 12"/30 cm., zippered pajama bag for night dress. Also to use as arm puppet. Dralon, in use as early as 1957, synthetic fiber fill, glass eyes with white iris, open felt mouth, grey felt claws, original blue ribbon. Shelf price $15.50 in 1964. Not in great demand but rare. Courtesy Susan Roeder. $175.00.

"Jolly Cockie", large arm puppet, 15½"/50 cm., No. 3486/50, a new item 1973-75, life-like dralon black and white cocker, typified by having all four legs and tail. In 1973 arm puppets were produced for the "puppet theater". Steiff has created many different puppet series over the years. Jolly Cockie and Jolly Lamb had a limited production. (Author). $150.00-175.00.

Hand Puppets: Cat, 6"/17 cm., mohair plush, straw head, green glass eyes, rose floss nose and claws, ear button/I.D. tag, "Made in Austria". Cockie dog, 6"/17 cm., short white mohair, long pile brown mohair ears, brown glass eyes. Older than cat. Available 1957-on. Courtesy Susan Roeder. $25.00 each.

Wooden pull toy "Zebra", 8"/20 cm. high, 6½"/18 cm. iong, No. 8360/18, highly polished beechwood, wood burned design. Brass plate embedded into body, "Steiff" in script with bear's head. A total of 12 different animals on red wooden wheels were produced from 1969-74. Of these the zebra is the most striking. Courtesy Kay Bransky. $45.00.